Adrian Masters is the Political Editor of ITV Cymru Wales. He presents the weekly political programme, 'Sharp End', and hosts live Leaders' Debates and election coverage. In recent years he's also become an unlikely TV chef with the programme 'Adrian's Welsh Bites' in which he makes a meal with the person that he's interviewing. He has twenty-five years' experience as a broadcast journalist and has been a reporter and presenter in both radio and television.

NOTHING HAS CHANGED

The 2017 Election Diaries

Adrian Masters

Parthian, Cardigan SA43 1ED
www.parthianbooks.com
First published in 2017
© Adrian Masters 2017
ISBN 978-1-912109-75-3
Edited by Gary Raymond
Cover Design by Alison Evans
Typeset by Elaine Sharples
Printed by Lightning Source
Published with the financial support of the Welsh Books Council
British Library Cataloguing in Publication Data
A cataloguing record for this book is available from the British Library.

INTRODUCTION

'Nothing has changed. Nothing has changed.' That's what Theresa May kept saying on a small stage in the small Memorial Hall at Gresford near Wrexham. Specifically it was her response to claims that she was making a U-turn on her disastrous manifesto pledge on paying for social care in England. But it became symbolic of wider changes that, when the election results finally came in on June the 9th, left her without a Commons majority.

In some senses nothing was changed by the election. She remained Prime Minister and Jeremy Corbyn remained in charge of Labour which remained in opposition in Westminster and in government in Wales. Plaid Cymru breathed a sigh of relief and celebrated gaining a seat but breakthrough remained elusive. The Liberal Democrats still weren't doing very well. Brexit talks continued as did the uncertainty surrounding them.

In every important respect though, everything changed. The Conservatives were heading towards historic gains and Labour was heading towards historic losses. They swapped places. Theresa May's authority was hopelessly hollowed out while her defeated opponent Jeremy Corbyn was invigorated and empowered by a party that was swollen with enthusiastic new supporters and, more surprisingly, voters. In Wales, Carwyn Jones used internal party turmoil and structural changes to build an unprecedented role for the Welsh party that seems unlikely to be overturned. Meanwhile Welsh Conservatives howled with rage at being left out of a campaign that had even bigger problems.

I haven't known a time like it in the quarter of a century I've been working as a journalist. Day after day, sometimes minute by minute, I've watched politics change in front of me. Certainties have been lost, rules bent or broken and leaders have risen and fallen.

It's the most remarkable time to be a political journalist which is a remarkable and unusual job at any time. It puts me in the most privileged position, a close eye-witness to events with the opportunity to hear what's happening directly from the mouths of those shaping, or trying to shape, the action.

I remember seeing the face of the First Minister, stony and confused in the hour after polling closed in 2015, disbelieving the exit poll, convinced it must be wrong. It wasn't. Then the same First Minister on election night this year, just as confused but in an entirely different mood as another accurate exit poll sank in. 'It must be young people,' he told me. 'I saw more young people at polling stations than ever before.'

I remember standing on a street in a Glasgow estate with Stephen Crabb, then Secretary of State for Wales, when he told me that, whatever the result, the Scottish referendum was a game changer in terms of the way the UK was governed. 'This changes everything,' he said. Neither of us knew quite how much politics would change after that moment.

I remember seeing David Cameron and his children eating ice creams at the Royal Welsh show. On another occasion, I made him sigh in an interview when I repeatedly asked him when his government would make a long-delayed decision on tax and borrowing powers for the Welsh Government. 'We have to get this right,' he said eventually. 'I don't have a date for you today.'

I remember standing outside the Senedd chamber when, for a moment, it looked like Leanne Wood might overturn rules and expectations and become First Minister. She can't do that, some said. Maybe not, but she certainly tried.

My journalism isn't the sort that weaves in commentary. I don't take a position, I don't think as many do, that I'm some sort of unofficial opposition. My job is simply to try to make politics clear and accessible to the ITV viewers, to challenge the politicians on behalf of those viewers, to report on what governments do and say, what opposition parties do and say and what they all do and say about each other. That's it. There's a need for commentator journalists but that's not my role and there's a big part of me that was relieved not to have to join the chorus of apologies coming from those who insisted such an outcome or another was inevitable in 2017.

It's a job that requires a lot of talking and, having missed the glory days of long, boozy lunches, a lot of coffee. It's about sharing and keeping confidences. There's a lot of information that I can't broadcast, for time reasons or because it's only of interest to a handful of people, or it's spin, or incorrect or superseded by events or, quite often, told me on a confidential basis.

I keep a lot of notes in my red notebooks – mostly scrawled in haste and often when I'm standing up or on the move, so they're as difficult to read as a GP's prescription. When I was asked to consider publishing an election diary, I began keeping fuller notes with more emphasis on remembering whole or nearly whole sentences for quoting. I also kept notes on my phone along with emails and texts. Honesty compels me to state that I didn't keep a diary in the sense that I didn't write up each entry as presented here at the end of each day. What I've done is to bring the notes of conversations, some private and some public, together with the texts, emails, tweets and whatsapp messages into the form of a diary. I hope by doing so it gives a sense of the exciting pace at which events unfolded as I saw them. Reporting on politics is a messy, often chaotic job. This account, I hope, shows just how much that's true and how it's as fun as that sounds.

This is the election campaign as seen by me. It's a privileged position to view it from, about as close as you can get without joining a political party and with a considerably wider frame. However, this isn't an attempt to give a comprehensive analysis of the campaign and I don't claim to cover every event: for instance I missed most of the manifesto launches in Wales. On occasion I pass on what colleagues told me who were at those events or covered other parts of the campaign. At other times, they remain a blank. This is my account of what I saw, what I was told and what I made of it.

It offers a snapshot of my job and hopefully gives some sense of what it's like to be a political journalist in these chaotic times. I'm grateful to ITV Cymru Wales for giving me the chance to do that job and for letting me write about it here as well as to quote from programmes I and others made during the campaign.

Accompanying my diary account are inserts looking more closely at certain aspects that have been written more recently and with hindsight. Since the election I've spoken to many of those who were intimately involved in the campaign to fill in some of the gaps. MPs, AMs, candidates and activists, advisers and strategists have all spoken to me with candour to help me develop a fuller picture of what went on.

My kind of political journalism relies on trust and talking to people. I respect confidentiality and when my sources don't want to be identified, I've respected that too. I've used neutral pronouns to make them harder to identify. The criticism will always be levelled by some that that approach makes me complicit with those politicians. I'm of the view that the information is more important than naming names and I have to trust that my record of fairness speaks for itself.

In these highly-charged and polarised times, it seems unfashionable to remain neutral. To me it's central and not just a convenient journalistic defence. The longer I do this job, the harder it seems to me to consider committing myself to one political view or another. It strikes me that the best service I can offer a confused public is to be scrupulously fair. It strikes me too that the pressure to comment or offer opinion as part of our journalism is what has led many journalists into the unfortunate position of having to apologise for getting things wrong. The urge to state in absolute terms that you know what's going to happen is difficult to resist. 2017 has shown that anything can happen and long may that last.

PROLOGUE

I decided to go for a walk and ended up behind a police cordon, caught up in the security operation following one of the most shocking terrorist attacks the UK has seen.

I'd been sitting in Portcullis House in Westminster, in the large atrium where MPs and their staff eat, drink and mingle. It's also a good place for journalists to bump into MPs to swap gossip and pick up possible stories. I'd been there for a while and had spoken to a few people but I wasn't working on a particular story and wasn't due to appear on our news programme at 6pm so I thought I'd stretch my legs. Since I was where I was, I walked over Westminster Bridge and onto the Southbank where crowds of tourists seemed to fill every available inch of space. I went into the Southbank Centre and started to head back.

On my way out, I looked down at my phone. Keith Phillips who was editing the programme that day had sent an email simply headed, 'U ok? Tell us all about it?'

I replied, 'About what?' Then I checked twitter.

My phone records show that I replied to Keith's email at 14:52. Twelve minutes earlier a car drove deliberately into people crossing the river. I looked in horror at the pictures people were tweeting of the very side of the bridge I'd just walked across. As I fought my way back towards it, I first heard the sirens and saw the blue lights. Realising that it was closed I turned around and half-walked, half-ran towards Waterloo bridge, crossed the river there and walked along the embankment towards Westminster. Roads near the bridge were already closed, so I cut through into Whitehall and towards Downing Street. I could go no further. Hundreds of people were crammed behind the police cordon there. Then there were shouts from the police, 'Has anyone dropped a rucksack? Does anyone recognise this rucksack?'

The cordon was moved and we were pushed back further and further still. By now I realised that I was unlikely to make it back to ITV's Millbank office.

My newsdesk colleagues in Cardiff were trying to find a way of taking me live into the news programme but that became increasingly unlikely. Meanwhile I and the hundreds of other people I was among were being pushed back up Whitehall toward Trafalgar Square. I tweeted some pictures of the scene. Not long afterwards I had a call from Geraint Evans, who's Special Adviser to the Welsh Secretary Alun Cairns, offering me sanctuary in Gwydyr House, the Georgian house which is the Whitehall base of the Wales Office. The cordon was now some way past that point so a police officer escorted me to the front door where I was welcomed by Allan Ross, the department's Head of Communications. He made me a cup of tea and gave me a biscuit and a seat. The staff were all watching the news channels and looking out the windows at the unfolding events. I'll always be grateful for that chance to rest, cool down, drink tea and make phone calls.

There was the possibility of finding an ITV Network News

crew which was in the area to see if they could help me send a live or as-live report to Cardiff so I thanked the Wales Office staff and left, leaving the locked-down Gwydyr House and walking across an oddly deserted Whitehall to duck beneath the cordon and back into the crowds.

I couldn't see the ITN crew but while I was standing there a young man came up to introduce himself. He was from Newport and recognised me from a conference that I'd chaired recently. He'd been here to attend the youth parliament and had walked out of Westminster tube station into the immediate aftermath of the attack, witnessing the blood and bodies on the ground. With no camera operator, I recorded an interview with him on my phone and sent it to Cardiff. Overseas journalists nearby realised he was an eyewitness and grabbed him for interviews too.

I tried to process what had happened. I was getting a lot of calls and texts from colleagues, family and friends checking that I was safe. But I felt a fraud. I hadn't been near the incident itself, I was safe and behind the cordon at all times. But I'd come so close. I didn't like to think what would have happened if I'd decided to go for my walk ten minutes later.

What happened that afternoon in Westminster and later in Manchester and London Bridge added fear and uncertainty to an already highly-charged election campaign. Security was tightened, not just at Parliament but at the Assembly and elsewhere. Questions about security and defence became a big part of the campaign itself.

And what an extraordinary campaign. What I hope this election diary shows more than anything is how events unfolded and how things changed. That's the main point. Hindsight commentators may say the outcome was always clear. It wasn't. My account shows how even right up to the end, and even as some things were becoming clear – the unpopularity of the Conservative manifesto and the popularity of Labour's along with changing perceptions of Theresa May and Jeremy Corbyn – many candidates, seasoned campaigners and senior figures within the parties still thought they knew what the outcome would be: a large Tory majority in the UK, with gains at the expense of Labour including in Wales.

I don't believe our first poll was wrong and neither do any of those in the political parties that I've spoken to since, even if they doubted the size of the Conservative lead it suggested. It may have seemed unlikely that the Conservatives would win twenty-one seats in Wales but they were on course to make historic gains. They thought so, Labour thought so and so did many within the other parties. There have been a lot of *mea culpa*s written by journalists for failing to spot what happened. I won't be making any apology for reporting what our polls told me at the start of the campaign because they echoed what I was being told by the people I was talking to. As the campaign progressed, it became clear things were changing in Wales as well as in the UK.

What changed? In Wales, it's clear that the policy of playing up 'Welsh Labour' paid off. Carwyn Jones saw his popularity remain strong throughout. The manifesto was more Welsh than ever before. A long-fought-for strategy of ensuring a role for Carwyn Jones at Labour's crucial Clause V meeting to finalise the UK manifesto also paid off and the party is now committed to positions on, for instance, devolution of policing that it's long resisted. There's no doubt in my mind that the tributes to Rhodri Morgan also cemented the view of Welsh Labour being different. Certainly at least one Conservative cabinet member agrees with me. But it would be a huge mistake to think that it was just the Welsh Labour brand that won it in Wales. The Corbyn surge clearly transformed Labour's fortunes here, leading more than one senior figure to muse ruefully about what they could have achieved if they'd put more resources into Preseli Pembrokeshire or Arfon.

There's no doubt in my mind either that the Conservatives squandered historic levels of support they'd built up. They weren't wasting their time in Bridgend, Wrexham or the two Newport constituencies. They were theirs for the taking and they lost them through a mixture of hubris and complacency, a failure to respond to the Labour surge and in a handful of constituencies, a heavy-handed approach to selection.

The mistakes of the Tories' UK campaign are being dissected by others although some of those mistakes will become clear in my account as they emerge in the period covered by this diary. They're familiar by now: an overly-centralised campaign putting too much emphasis on a leader who wasn't comfortable being the centre of attention.

And that manifesto. On election night when I asked a senior Labour figure when things changed, he said it was immediately after the manifesto was published, adding that, 'I can't believe it was just the manifesto.' Many Conservatives think it was. I asked the same question of a senior Tory MP who said the change was almost instantaneous and visible from the day after the manifesto publication. For those who think manifestos and campaigns don't make any difference, 2017 will be food for thought.

It's also important to remember that this election came in the midst of a huge amount of change and uncertainty.

Since 2014 there has been an independence referendum in Scotland followed by a surge in support for the SNP; a UK General Election which the Conservatives surprised everyone including themselves by winning; a Welsh election which brought UKIP members into the Assembly and left Labour without a majority and facing a Sliding Doors moment when Leanne Wood almost replaced Carwyn Jones as First Minister (although for how long is another matter); and another referendum that saw British voters decide to leave the European Union with all the upheaval that that entails.

Along the way, polls and pollsters have gone from being treated as infallible sages to quack doctors peddling snake oil; a Conservative Prime Minister and Chancellor have not only lost a referendum, but lost office and left parliament while the party changed leaders swiftly and brutally; the Labour party has publicly displayed its deep divisions in two leadership elections; one party (UKIP) has risen with seemingly unstoppable momentum only to fall apart once its objective was gained while another (the Liberal Democrats) has fallen from sharing government to the edge of extinction.

In Wales the kaleidoscope has kept on shifting.

Labour continued to dominate Assembly politics but the election of 2016, the change in the party's UK leadership and the Brexit vote clearly altered dynamics in Cardiff Bay. The last two emboldened Carwyn Jones and others to push forward the 'Welsh Labour' strategy of differentiating the party in Wales from the party at a UK level. A fiction in many ways since both continue as one organisation with no separate funding or administration, the tactic had been started by Rhodri Morgan and taken up enthusiastically by Carwyn Jones despite scepticism from some Welsh Labour MPs and derision by opponents who sometimes called it 'Diet Plaid'. Previously less willing to engage in UK politics, 2016 and 2017 also saw him become much more active on the UK stage, perhaps emulating and certainly working with his Scottish counterpart, Nicola Sturgeon.

The Welsh Conservatives had a good election in 2015 followed by disappointment in 2016 and occasional public infighting. Plaid Cymru may not have seen an SNP-style surge but promoted its policies by doing deals with Labour and celebrated a famous victory in Rhondda. The Liberal Democrats paid the price for the 2010 coalition with successively worse election results culminating in losing all but Kirsty Williams in the Assembly, a position they thought couldn't get any worse. UKIP arrived in Cardiff Bay in a burst of enthusiasm and outrage.

Assembly politics refused to settle down after May 2016. The last remaining Lib Dem, Kirsty Williams, joined the Welsh Government as Education Secretary. UKIP's leader in Wales, Nathan Gill, fell out with the rest of his group when he was ousted by Neil Hamilton. He became an independent AM. A second UKIP member, Mark Reckless, followed but semi-joined the Welsh Conservatives, a move which caused huge tensions within the party. Plaid Cymru's former leader, Dafydd Elis-Thomas, quit the group and the party, sitting as an independent but promising to support Labour for the duration of the Assembly, giving Carwyn Jones his majority at last.

It had already been a time of extraordinary change and upheaval by April 2017. And then Theresa May went walking in Snowdonia.

'The advantage of the method is that it sweeps
up accidentally several stray matters which I
should exclude if I hesitated, but which
are the diamonds of the dustheap.'
VIRGINIA WOOLF, *A Writer's Diary*

'Certainly you can define a journalist as someone
who passes on: a compulsion to blab and spill
secrets is one of the few things everyone in
journalism would agree is essential.'
ANDREW MARR, *My Trade*

TUESDAY 18TH APRIL

The letter is printed on pink paper. It bears the Royal Coat of Arms and in large lettering the words 'Jury Summons.' 'You have been selected for jury service,' it says and I must attend at 9am on June the 5th. I've never served on a jury before and I'm quite intrigued by what it involves. I doubt there'll be much going on that week, so having discussed with Nick[1] the implications for my news commitments and for presenting Sharp End I tick the box to say 'no' to a deferral, put the form in the envelope and leave it on the table to post later.

It being the day after Easter Monday, I'm trying to take a week's leave need to go out and about to run some errands. A Welsh

---

[1] Nick Powell, head of politics at ITV Cymru Wales

Labour person texts me asking, 'Any idea what TM's announcement is?' I have to answer honestly that I don't and that I'd been hoping for a quiet week off. My contact's speculation is this: 'Two most likely scenarios seem to be early GE or direct rule in N Ireland. MPs and even frontbenchers don't seem to have as much of a clue as the rest of us.' I respond, 'Part of me hopes for an early election but I think it might finish me off!' The reply comes back: 'You and the Labour Party!'

Next comes a text from Nick saying, 'Election rumour underway. May making "important announcement" at 11.15.' This is backed up by an email from the news desk sharing an alert from colleagues in the network newsroom. My week off is about to end.

I switch on the car radio and hear the Prime Minister in Downing Street saying that, 'The country is coming together but Westminster is not,' and that she will aim to hold a General Election on June 8th.

Back at home, I take the jury service summons out of its envelope, cross out the tick and hastily write an explanation that I imagine will appear highly unlikely to whichever official reads it. I write that a snap election has just been called for the week that I've been summoned, that as Political Editor I will be expected to cover it and please could I request a deferral. I seal the envelope, post it and hope for the best.

Soon I'm on a train to London, looking at news on my phone, twitter and emails showing that everyone else is also coming to terms with what's happening.

In an interview with Robert Peston, Theresa May reveals that she changed her mind about holding an early election when she was on a walking holiday in Snowdonia with her husband. Perhaps there was something about the scenic grandeur that made her think that what Britain needs most is 'Certainty and stability.'

All the signs are that she'll get that certainty. The latest YouGov poll puts the Conservatives on 44% with Labour on just 23%. She may well deny, as she does in the Peston interview, that she's playing political games but for her party that lead and the chance to cause further damage to an already divided Labour party must be irresistible.

The reactions start arriving in my inbox. They're pretty much as I expect although the one surprise comes from Plaid Cymru leader Leanne Wood. In a series of interviews she makes it clear that she's at least thinking about becoming more closely involved in this election than she'd already be as leader, possibly standing for the Rhondda. Winning the seat in last year's Assembly election was an astonishing achievement for Plaid Cymru and herself, but standing for Parliament is fraught with risks. However, it's a sign of what an extraordinary election this is going to be. She tells my colleague Rob Osborne that, 'I'm not ruling anything in or anything out at this point in time.'

I get to Westminster at around 4.30. While I've been travelling my colleagues in Cardiff and Millbank have arranged for a couple of live slots and an interview with the Welsh Secretary.

Earlier I'd had time to alter the jury service summons, change into a suit and throw a few things into a bag but not enough time to shave so go on air with four days' stubble.

Andrea[2] hands to me and I say, 'If I weren't your political editor, Andrea, and old enough to know better, I'd start by saying OMG – it's that surprising a decision. There must be something in the Snowdonia water because Theresa May has repeatedly said that there wouldn't be a General Election, despite all the speculation. Today she said there would be.'

I put that point to Alun Cairns, asking him why anyone should believe a word of his and the Prime Minister's after those repeated denials. He says, 'The Prime Minister and the government didn't want to be in this position but we've seen how the parliamentary process is being used to frustrate the debates in parliament and to frustrate the negotiations.'

Andrea asks me why I think the Prime Minister has changed her mind and I say, 'Brexit and politics which are intertwined.' The politics is that Theresa May calculates that the Conservatives are likely to do well and Labour will do badly. In the process, she thinks she'll strengthen her hand for the Brexit negotiations.

I refer to Leanne Wood's refusal to rule herself out as a potential candidate and say, 'To be honest, in this election, I wouldn't rule anything out.'

---

[2] Andrea Byrne, Presenter ITV Cymru Wales news

A Mistake By Theresa May?

Most Conservatives that I've spoken to since the election agree that calling a snap election was not just a surprise but a mistake by Theresa May. One senior MP told me how disappointed they were because it meant that with the Brexit process barely underway after the triggering of Article 50, 'we were going to waste a couple of months having an election that we didn't need because we already had an overall majority. I've been around long enough to know that you can't take anything for granted and I was concerned that what actually did happen might happen.

'I had doubts about her campaigning ability and also I just couldn't understand how we were going to put into place an election-ready machine in the time we had available. It seemed to me we had no advantage over the opposition. Unless we'd been doing a lot of the work in the meantime to put together manifesto and materials we needed, which we clearly hadn't.'

But at least one senior Conservative that I've spoken to since can't forget how it was at the beginning of the campaign. 'It was amazing. The first few days of campaigning, the positive response to Theresa May was like nothing I've ever seen. You didn't even need to finish her full name. You could knock the door and say, 'Hi I'm calling on behalf of There...' and they're like yeah, I'm with you. She's great. I'm so pleased she's called the election because she's absolutely fantastic.' That was pretty much the first week of the campaign. At that point it was absolutely the right thing to do.'

The snap election may have taken many by surprise even though it had been a source of speculation. But it may have been planned earlier than thought. In fact some I've spoken to are convinced that the Prime Minister decided as early as January and only finalised her decision when she went walking in Snowdonia at Easter.

WEDNESDAY 19TH APRIL

Theresa May needs to win the support of two thirds of MPs to get around the Fixed-term Parliaments Act which was supposed to ensure parliaments always last five years. She succeeds, with just thirteen MPs voting against the motion, one of whom is Cynon Valley MP, Ann Clwyd.

ITV network has confirmed it will hold a debate which is good news for our plan to broadcast a Wales debate. However, Theresa May has said she won't take part. Leanne Wood is quoted as saying the Prime Minister should be 'empty-chaired if she doesn't show up to any planned TV debates.' I wonder how May's refusal will affect things in Wales. Will Alun Cairns be under pressure not to take part too in order not to show up his boss or will they consider them separately?

My report for Wales at Six begins: 'Change is the new normal in politics. Upheaval is happening nearly every day.'

As always when there's a major political event, Abingdon Green fills up with cameras, gazebos, trestle tables and journalists. Overhead a helicopter circles. In my report I say, 'You can sense the excitement here in Westminster, you can hear it certainly. You can see that everybody's waiting. They're waiting for something that's going to happen in there that's going to change British politics at a time when it's already changing, day by day it seems.'

Plaid Cymru MP Hywel Williams gives me an upbeat assessment, seeing the volatile political situation and Brexit itself as an opportunity for Wales to change. 'This is a turning point for Wales and we want to seize the opportunity.'

I put it to Labour MP Jo Stevens that this election has come at a bad time for her party because it's divided. 'Not in Wales we're not,' she says.

In my report I call the snap election Theresa May's Easter Surprise, and proudly maintain the seasonal language by adding that MPs have now decided to spring a summer election.

Live on air I note that some parties are worried and some see it as an opportunity. I add that, 'All I'll say is that everything has changed. Again.'

THURSDAY 20TH APRIL

I go back to trying to take time off but it's impossible not to follow what's happening.

Owain has been out campaigning with Carwyn Jones.[3] The camera catches one of those doorstep confrontation moments when a voter tells the Welsh Labour leader, 'I just think you're a spent force. You haven't got the passion any more.' As Owain points out in his report, Welsh Labour must be hoping that's not

---

[3] Owain Phillips, Political Reporter at ITV Cymru Wales

a widespread view as it puts the First Minister at front and centre of its campaign.

Asked if he thinks Jeremy Corbyn is an asset, Carwyn Jones says, 'He has to prove himself. He's still fairly new as a leader in an election campaign. I think people want to hear an alternative; they're fed up of the same old same old from the Tories.'

Also in Owain's report Alun Cairns, campaigning in Wrexham, says, 'People here in Wrexham want that security and that leadership that Theresa May is showing so therefore there are key areas like this that are battlegrounds that we think have the prospect of becoming Conservative.'

FRIDAY 21ST APRIL

Jeremy Corbyn is visiting Cardiff North. Owain's report for Wales at Six shows a huge crowd treating the Labour leader like a rock star. 'Their Elvis, their McCartney, their Bowie', as Owain puts it.

It looks pretty chaotic but Owain manages to get a word with the leader, asking him his message to uncertain Remain voters. Corbyn insists that he 'will get an agreement with the EU to protect jobs... and a good relationship with Europe in the future.'

Nick texts to say, 'The poll on Monday will show the Conservatives ahead.' What a way to start the campaign.

"We're Fucked"

Labour was in terrible trouble at the beginning of the election campaign. Our first poll may have raised eyebrows when it showed Labour ten points behind and in danger of failing to win a majority of seats in Wales for the first time in a century but Labour people then and now, as well as those in other parties, believe that it fairly reflected the scale of the problems they faced even if some were hopeful they could shrink the gap over the course of the campaign.

They didn't need to rely on our poll or their own guesswork either. With the local elections due to take place in May, Labour in Wales was already in campaign mode and those in Transport House in Cardiff who were poring over canvassing returns could see the terrible reality of the situation.

'The overarching feel was one of 'We're fucked,' one senior member of the campaign team told me. 'The feedback from the doorstep was grim. There was an absolute and unshakeable belief on behalf of many of the Welsh PLP that they were toast. You even had long-standing Welsh Parliamentary colleagues gifting their offices at the end of the session because they thought wouldn't be reoccupying them. There was an absolute sense that we were in big trouble and this absolutely wasn't finger in the wind stuff.'

Those on the left agree that the party was in a bad way although they put the situation down to relentlessly negative press coverage and public rows between MPs. One prominent Welsh Corbyn supporter said to me that, 'The onslaught in the media and divisions

25

in the party meant that a lot of the traditional Labour loyalty vote was impacted by the barrage.'

The Corbyn team was more optimistic that the situation could be turned around and believe what later became known as the Corbyn surge began much earlier than is acknowledged by others in the party. Those close to the leader point to the rally in Whitchurch in Cardiff at the beginning of the campaign when hundreds turned up at short notice to see the leader speak as a sign that even early on there was an enthusiasm for Corbyn and his type of politics. They say too that the largest increase in the polls was the four point average that happened in the first ten days. There was then another surge in the two weeks from mid-May before the polls began to level off and reach a plateau in the final week. For both those reasons they reject the notion that the Corbyn surge was an end-of-campaign surprise. To say that, I've been told, is 'reverse engineering' to cover the embarrassment of those who failed to recognise earlier what was happening in areas where there was a lot of young voters and to act on it.

For many on the left that I've spoken to, even that optimism only stretched to retaining the same number of seats, not making any gains. Those running the campaign in Wales saw it as defensive from beginning to end. As one official put it, 'Even in the exit poll the extrapolation had us losing seats in the North East and put us fifty-fifty in one of the Newports. So I don't think there was ever a point where we thought, this is in the bag, it's fine. There was a genuine belief there was a risk.'

That risk was caused to a very large extent by Jeremy Corbyn's unpopularity, particularly in Labour's heartland areas where traditional

Labour supporters lived. Many, particularly older white men, were telling canvassers and candidates that 'Jeremy Corbyn is rubbish.'

'There was a lot of anger,' a senior member of the campaign team told me. 'I'm talking about heartland seats here. There were a lot of reports coming back that Jeremy was a genuine issue on the doorstep. Certainly, early doors, some of the Tory attacks on him were landing home. We were hearing 'people don't like him and people are not going to vote for us' and that was an issue clearly identified.'

It wasn't just the leader though that was causing problems. It was a perception that the party was divided. Potential voters offered a list of concerns ranging from the leader's appearance to his controversial public positions before he became leader on defence and law and order matters. They were worried too about the UK leadership generally and the public fallings out between MPs. 'The Labour brand', they were hearing, was tainted.

MONDAY 24TH APRIL

An early start to digest the implications of the poll. It's even more shocking than I first thought, showing that the Conservatives are on an incredible 40% in Wales, up twelve on the 2015 result which itself was a pretty good one for them. Even more astonishing, Labour are ten points behind at 30%. In our last poll, Labour was on 33% in Wales and that was the lowest it had been at since 2010.

Roger Scully joins us to run through the figures.[4] His projection

----

[4] Professor Roger Scully from Cardiff University's Wales Governance Centre. The Welsh Political Barometer Poll is jointly commissioned by ITV Cymru Wales and the Centre and carried out by YouGov.

is that the Conservatives would win twenty-one of Wales' forty seats. Labour would hold onto just fifteen, Plaid Cymru would keep its current three and the Liberal Democrats just the one they hold now. The ten Labour seats which would turn Conservative in this scenario are: Bridgend, Wrexham, Cardiff South and Penarth, Delyn, Alyn and Deeside, Newport West, Ynys Môn, Newport East, Cardiff West and Cardiff South and Penarth.

Roger drops stunning statistic after stunning statistic while we sip our coffees. He jokes that the last time the Tories led in Wales was the 50s. Pause. The 1850s. The last time Labour didn't come first in Wales, he says, was in Lloyd George's Coupon Election of 1918. 1931 was the last time Labour didn't win half the seats in Wales. And 2015 was the twentieth General Election in a row when Labour won a majority. It would be an astonishing collapse for the party in Wales.

Other aspects are interesting. It seems the Brexit referendum has changed the way people vote. The Conservatives appear to be hoovering up two thirds of those who voted UKIP in 2015. Most of those will have been Leave voters and a lot of them were Labour voters. The poll data, as others have, shows that most current Labour voters are strongly in favour of Remain which suggests that Leavers have already left Labour. If this is anywhere near the true picture, it would seem that the link with Labour has snapped for Labour supporters who voted UKIP in 2015, then voted Leave in 2016. Now the Conservatives and Theresa May have come to own Brexit so it seems likely Labour Leavers are thinking about trusting the Tories to deliver it.

The figures where people were asked to rate party leaders out of 10 show that Jeremy Corbyn is unpopular but no more so than Tim Farron. It's just that Theresa May is amazingly popular. 4.9 for a Tory in Wales is pretty unusual and politicians anywhere rarely average more than 5.

We're all nervous in case it's a rogue poll. Roger says it's in keeping with GB-wide polls so less likely to be an outlier. We have two other polls planned before the election. We discuss whether or not to commission more. A decision is taken to commission another two so that there'll be four before the election.

In an article to accompany the figures on our website, Roger has written:

Something extraordinary could be about to happen. Wales is on the brink of an electoral earthquake. The Conservatives appear to be on course to win the majority of Welsh parliamentary seats for the first time in the democratic era, while Labour faces losing a general election in Wales for the first time since 1918.

Just before it's published I tweet: 'Take a deep breath.'

Soon afterwards I receive a text from someone well-connected with the Conservative Party at a UK level saying, 'Owen Smith has to shoulder some of the blame for that Welsh poll. Of course the only poll that counts is the one on Election Day. (But just between you and I ... bloody hell!)'

I have a phone conversation with Geraint who's warily delighted, saying that it's hard to believe.[5] He says he'll talk to Number 10 and Alun Cairns and get me a quote. Before it arrives, an email comes in with a response from Andrew RT Davies: *...such polls come with a serious health warning, given the industry's failure to predict recent results. What we can be sure of, however, is the outstanding performance of the Prime Minister, who offers strong and stable leadership.*

In his statement Carwyn Jones says the poll contains a warning for his party: 'We know Jeremy needs to prove himself to the electorate here in Wales, just as we know the political weather is tough going, a fact underlined by the polling numbers released today.'

A former Labour minister however, says the warning is starker. Leighton Andrews tweets: 'More evidence that Jeremy Corbyn should resign asap.'[6]

Plaid Cymru's Simon Thomas replies to my tweet saying, 'Not a shock to anyone who's been canvassing and there will be local factors, but Corbyn is destroying Labour.' Plaid's formal response is: 'This poll is a glimpse of a future which could await Wales. If the Tories do win on these numbers, the future of our nation is at risk.'

In Wales at Six, we run Pathé footage of the National Government victory in 1931, the last time Labour didn't win most seats in Wales. In the studio I describe the poll as 'stunning' and say that, 'If it were to become real it would be a truly historic shift.'

---

[5] Geraint Evans, Special Adviser to the Secretary of State for Wales, Alun Cairns.

[6] Former Labour minister who lost his Rhondda seat in 2016

My next Welsh Bites programme is broadcast this evening.[7] This week's chef is the athlete-turned-peer, Baroness Tanni Grey-Thompson who has an amazing story to tell of determination and drive. It's a story which she tells with great humour as she demonstrates when she tweets to me, 'chef is a bit of a strong word.' She cheerfully admits to cooking little other than the most basic dishes, so we'd talked and laughed in her London flat while we threw together a vegetable stir fry using a frying pan because she couldn't find her wok. I knew her a little from my early years in journalism and we got on like a house on fire during the filming. Whether or not you're for or against the House of Lords, she's a great advert for the benefits of people from outside traditional party backgrounds being involved in politics.

An email arrives from the former leader of Plaid Cymru and former Deputy First Minister in the Labour-Plaid coalition Welsh Government, Ieuan Wyn Jones. He's going to put his name forward as a potential candidate for Ynys Môn, the constituency he represented first as an MP and then as an AM.

It's an interesting development. As a well-known and well-liked figure on Anglesey, he must have a good chance although island politics don't follow any recognisable rules.

----

[7] 'Adrian's Welsh Bites' in which, unlikely as it seems, I get to interview people with a high public profile whilst cooking dinner with them. It sprang from an original series focussing on leaders of the main parties standing in the Assembly election of 2016. This second series expanded the guest list from politics to well-known faces such as Tanni, Colin Jackson and Simon Weston.

On Sharp End, the Conservative AM Nick Ramsay tells me that whatever the truth behind the poll, 'There is something happening out there. There is a movement and I think the Labour party should be worried and the Conservatives do have grounds for optimism.'

On her party's poll problems, Christina Rees echoes Carwyn Jones' previous admission that, 'We've got a mountain to climb and we never pretended it's not going to be a struggle.'

UKIP's Neil Hamilton states that by the weekend his party hopes to have a candidate in every one of the forty constituencies here in Wales. He confirms that he'll be a candidate in Carmarthen East and Dinefwr.

TUESDAY 25TH APRIL

I head off for Bridgend and as I join the M4, I realise that the motorcade is sweeping by. I keep up with the flashing blue lights of the police cars and bikes that are in front and behind the Prime Minister's cars, thinking that at least I'd know which way to go once I turned off the motorway without using a satnav. It's surprising how you can soon be lulled into the rhythm of the convoy, something which is fine on the M4, but once we're on the streets approaching Brackla, I have to remind myself that I'm not part of it and, unlike the other vehicles, am supposed to obey traffic lights.

The community hall in Brackla is already full of Conservative activists. They're not all from Bridgend though: I recognise faces from all over South Wales. One man tells me approvingly that it's 'a good crowd,' adding, 'Not bad given that the invitation only went out last night. I got mine at half past ten.'

These are always surreal affairs and always involve a lot of waiting about, although Theresa May is developing a reputation for arriving early. About a hundred and fifty Conservatives are guided into a circle leaving a central space for a small platform. Some are given placards with the words 'Strong and stable leadership that's right for Britain' and a campaign official rehearses with them how and when to deploy them.

It's very hot in the hall, particularly as it fills up with activists and media. Lobby journalists cram into the area reserved for us which, it quickly becomes apparent, will be at the back of the crowd when it assembles. That's why, led by sketch writers Quentin Letts and John Crace, some of them drag chairs over and stand on them, to try to get a better view of the action. The activists are told to crowd around in a sort of circle, leaving a small gap around a small stage which is set up in the middle. That's where a handful of senior figures including Alun Cairns have gathered. I can't see how Theresa May makes her way through the tightly-packed crowd but when Alun Cairns introduces her she steps up onto the platform and addresses the crowd.

There's the usual discussion about which cameras are allowed in, who will act as 'pool' and 'pool cuts' – terms for the agreed sharing of footage of political events. Our camera woman, Lynsey, is 'pool cuts' so we lend a radio mic to a panicked Robert Nisbet from Sky News and Laura Kuenssberg from the BBC who aren't sure they'll get their questions recorded.

Parties tend to insist on certain rules for covering these events and mostly we play by them. I ask a Tory press officer if there's a protocol and he says 'just bob up' for a question. That's what I do once the Prime Minister has finished speaking but she follows a clearly pre-planned route of asking Kuenssberg, Robert Nisbet, the Sun, the Guardian and the Western Mail, leaving me looking like a schoolboy at the back of the class, repeatedly raising my hand. Lynn, who is acting as an extra camera has managed to capture my frustration so that I can use it in my news report later.[8]

----
[8] Lynn Courtney, Producer of Sharp End

There's a bit of history here. Since becoming Prime Minister Theresa May has made several visits to Wales. On her first, just days after taking the job, she met Carwyn Jones and granted only one 'pooled clip,' i.e a single question and answer, to the BBC to be shared with other media.

Her next visit was to a meeting of the Joint Ministerial Committee in Cardiff and there were no interviews for anyone.

Her third visit was to the Conservatives' spring forum in Cardiff. I joined other journalists trying to shout out questions as she arrived, with no expectation of an answer. There was no interview then either and so in frustration I tweeted that she'd made three visits to Wales without an interview.

I don't usually go in for media moaning but that tweet got a lot of attention in the right places. That night, a Friday, I received a call about her plan to visit Swansea the following Monday to agree the Swansea Bay City region deal. 'I saw your tweet,' said the Number 10 press officer and promised 'a couple of questions' on Monday.

'A couple of questions' usually means just that. David Cameron in particular was adept at walking away as he finished answering a second question. But that Monday, Theresa May and her press officer, let 'a couple of questions' develop into a hardly-expansive but still more generous than usual three or four minutes.

At the end of it I joked that every time she or anyone else talked about the 'Bay City region,' I thought about the Bay City Rollers. 'Me too,' she laughed and, laying her hand on my arm, added, 'That's exactly what I told this lot earlier.' I was quite surprised at that light-hearted and human note. She often seems a bit awkward in interview situations.

I'd also been surprised by her in October 2016 when I joined other ITV colleagues from across the UK in a series of short interviews at the Conservative conference in Manchester. These are a little like speed-dating: the interviewee sits in place while colleagues from the English regions, Scotland, Northern Ireland and I, swap places and get a strictly timed three and a half minutes.

When I sat down in Manchester I was surprised that she knew my name. Although I caught a glimpse later of the file in which I could see my picture at the top of a couple of pages of briefing notes, it's still noteworthy because it's unusual.

In my report, over pictures of the volunteers holding up placards with the slogan 'Strong and stable in the National Interest' I say, 'There's no missing the May message this election. Even the Prime Minister has it written on big cards for her to see.' I use a clip of her saying, 'That is what this election is about, about leadership, about stability, about doing the right thing for Britain.'

The shots of me reaching my hand up and turning to Lynn's camera, looking like a shamefaced schoolboy make it into the report. But I make a serious point that she does have questions to answer and will keep getting asked them. Others are beginning to note the stage-managed nature of these events. Without comment, I tweet the following: 'In Bridgend, for info, Theresa May accepted questions from BBC network, Sky, the Sun, the Guardian and Western Mail.'

I run a clip of Carwyn Jones saying, 'What have the Tories ever done for Wales? Absolutely nothing.'

Owain's report is from Plaid Cymru's launch on Anglesey. Their placards are in evidence as much as were those of the Conservatives but bear the slogan, 'Defending Wales.' Leanne Wood tells Owain that Plaid hopes to do well in Ynys Môn but also that there are 'other seats where we can do well.'

He's spoken to Albert Owen, an indefatigable campaigner whose main aim is to defy the odds. He tells Owain, 'It's always a tough seat... I'm always the underdog and I always win against the odds.'

In the studio I say that everything in this election campaign is accelerated and remark that it's all about momentum and demonstrating that momentum.

WEDNESDAY 26TH APRIL

I'm in Westminster. Walking through one of the back routes in parliament, amid fishy-smelling bins, smoking areas and delivery doors, I bump into a senior member of the government. Like most MPs he's carrying papers, folders and general stuff that needs to be cleared out of offices as parliament is prorogued. In his case they're in three or four large plastic bags for life, Sainsbury's I think. We stop to talk; he's gleeful but disbelieving of our poll although he's certain things are changing and is confident about gaining Bridgend and Newport West.

'Sensible Kippers are voting Tory,' he says. 'Not the mad lot, the racists; we don't want those. But the sensible ones are voting for us. And a lot of those were Labour voters.

'This is a crossroads moment,' he continues. 'Labour is institutionally hollowed out in Wales. Dislike of the Conservative-Lib

Dem coalition gave it a boost despite itself. Whether or not May wins, things have changed in Wales.'

As he walks off, he raises the bags for life in the air to wave and calls cheerfully back at me, 'I've waited a long time for this.'

I head up to the Press Gallery for Welsh Questions and Prime Minister's Questions. Referring to my now-public moaning about a lack of interview, a government press officer says, 'If I were you I'd be hacked off. If you want to woo Wales, don't piss off the commercial broadcaster.' He says the poll means that, 'they need you now that Wales is the new rock and roll.'

It's not just me who's frustrated at not getting a question. From where I am in the press gallery, I can see Swansea East MP Carolyn Harris repeatedly trying to catch the Speaker's eye. As Welsh Questions comes to a close, she looks up at me in the gallery and mimes stamping her feet and clenching her fists.

In Prime Minister's Questions, Theresa May brings back an old friend – criticism of the Welsh NHS. She taunts Jeremy Corbyn with 'Labour's custodianship of the NHS in Wales. There is somewhere the NHS is being cut – it's in Wales under the Labour party.' Corbyn doesn't rise to it this time although to be fair he has staunchly defended his Welsh colleagues against those attacks in interviews and elsewhere, something which Ed Miliband rarely did to the frustration of Welsh Labour leaders.

I text Labour contacts for a response. 'An outright lie,' is the terse reply.

After PMQs I bump into a couple of Conservative MPs. Both like the poll but worry it could cost them votes as supporters relax and think they don't need to turn out. 'I've been telling my lot it was close and I'll be scaring them till June the 8th,' said one. The other said, 'I don't believe the figures but something's going on.' Another Conservative that I speak to tells me, 'Bridgend is in play. Wrexham is in play. Twenty-one seats seems a bit OTT but Theresa May is trusted.'

Caerphilly MP Wayne David tells me that Carwyn Jones has asked him to chair the Welsh Labour campaign and to oversee the manifesto. I take this as another sign of how much Welsh Labour will play up its distance from Jeremy Corbyn because although he agreed to go back into the front bench team, Wayne David had previously been publicly critical of the Labour leader.

A Welsh Labour MP asks me, 'What's with your poll? I take it it's right. I shouldn't say it but Bridgend is gone – you've been there; it feels like a Tory seat.'

Our debate has now been confirmed for 17th May. It'll be two hours and in an outside venue yet to be arranged with an audience. One difference this time is that we're going to have VTs to introduce the people who'll ask the formal questions.

THURSDAY 27TH APRIL

I meet ITV's Director of News and Current Affairs, Michael Jermey on Westminster Bridge. He wants to know what's going on in Wales while I'm curious about the likelihood of a UK TV debate. He says it'll definitely go ahead but he's also pretty sure that Theresa May won't back down in her refusal to take part.

I meet a UK Government contact for coffee. I want to know if

Alun Cairns is likely to take part in our TV debate if the PM refuses to take part in others. I'm surprised to be told that that won't cause a problem but I'm warned that, 'We will have a problem if it's heavily weighted towards Assembly members and that means if Carwyn and Leanne are doing it. It should be parliamentary candidates. It should be Liz Saville-Roberts for Plaid. And where's Christina Rees in all this? Has she been put in a box?'[9]

I'm told to look out for a more hands-on approach to devolution that means 'the days of devolve and forget are gone. Yes, health is devolved but it doesn't mean we don't care about it. Economic development is devolved, but we still think it's important.'

I mention the question over repatriation of EU powers. It has to be done UK-wide. 'Are pharmaceutical companies going to accept four sets of regulations? What about fisheries? Fish don't respect devolved boundaries.' I can't help but feel this is going to set the UK Government on course for a row with the Welsh Government and other party leaders in Wales who think there should be straight repatriation of powers to Cardiff Bay.

Welsh Labour's press officer Rhiannon texts to say that, 'Just to let you know – on background – that you can expect an announce-ment about candidates this afternoon.' When I tell Nick about this he texts to say that the Conservatives have told him they'll have all candidates for target seats picked by Monday. They're moving quickly as they must.

A Conservative figure tells me that after the poll, 'lots of people

----
[9] Roberts, Plaid Cymru's Parliamentary Leader, MP for Dwyfor Meirionnydd; Rees, Shadow Welsh Secretary, MP for Neath

who are never interested in knocking doors have suddenly started asking if the party was looking for candidates and incredibly naming seats of preference. Fair weather friends,' says my contact, 'will always be around as long as people are looking for seats. Incredibly annoying.'

Matt Greenough calls to tell me that Carwyn Jones is giving a speech in London tonight.[10] He sends me an extract of the speech. In it, the First Minister is going to call for a 'better kind of election' which is apposite given that there's much talk about political insults today after Boris Johnson used a newspaper column to call Jeremy Corbyn a 'mutton-headed old mugwump.'

I'm more struck by this paragraph:

I hope the Prime Minister – after her visit to Wales this week – will sign up to a similar approach, and I invite her to debate with me on these terms, when she is back in Wales during the campaign.

A direct challenge from the First Minister to the Prime Minister to debate with him seems to me a good story so I arrange to meet him at the Daily Express offices where he's due to be interviewed.

It turns into more of an ordeal than I'd have liked. The Welsh Government team is delayed by appalling traffic from Paddington. It's very cold and it starts to rain in the hour and a half that I spend standing on the street swapping texts with an apologetic Jo Sabin.[11] Eventually the car crawls into view and frustrated by the still-heavy traffic, the First Minister and his team abandon the car and walk.

----
[10] Special Adviser to the First Minister
[11] Welsh Government press officer

This reminds me of the time I was waiting outside Bute House in Edinburgh where he was due to meet Nicola Sturgeon. On that occasion the weather was lovely and Carwyn Jones surprised and baffled Scottish Government press officers and waiting photographers by declining an offer of a car in favour of walking from the train station to Bute House.

In the past the First Minister has been a bit reluctant to dive into UK politics. That seems to be gone now. However, as a result of the delays we only have time for a short interview – I need to get the clips back to our Millbank studios and back to Cardiff in time for tonight's news. I'm also keen not to be rained on.

In the clip that I use, he says, 'I'm saying to the Prime Minister: You were in Bridgend at the beginning of the week. Come back and let's have a debate, you and me, and let's make sure people can test out the positions we take.' That's about as direct an involvement as you can get.

Late that night I receive a text from a UK Government contact: 'I see a guy who is not standing for election is challenging the PM to a debate!'

TV Debates

Since 2010 TV debates have become established parts of election campaigns even if the main thing they offer is pre-debate argument and controversy about who's involved and how they're arranged.

It's not clear how much effect they have on the campaign although they provide parties and journalists something to focus on. As one political adviser put it to me, they don't necessarily have an effect unless one of the participants has a car crash of a debate.

Before 2015 I'd chaired a lot of debates involving audiences and had presented a lot of live TV, including a lot of live and lively debate programmes. I'd never combined the two until I hosted that year's Welsh Leaders' Debate.

That year had seen another significant change. With mixed motives no doubt, David Cameron had insisted that the leaders of Plaid Cymru, the Scottish National Party and the Greens take part in the UK TV debates. It made them much bigger events and it had the effect of involving me more closely in the network debates, both in terms of covering them and being involved in the build-up and rehearsal process.

For our own debate a week or so later, I took my tone from the host of the first UK debate, Julie Etchingham, to make it more about moderating fairly and about keeping the leaders to time and not to see it as a series of interviews even though I needed to be ready to challenge.

Politicians are concerned about their cameras – most of them are primed by their teams to look directly at the camera, to speak directly to the viewer at home as much if not more than to the audience in the hall.

In 2015 I introduced Stephen Crabb for his closing statement when neither he nor the production team was expecting it. It meant the camera dedicated to him wasn't ready for the close-up. The director scrambled as quickly as possible and caught up with him a few seconds into his closing statement.

That was my fault but there's no room for error by those taking *part; the slightest slip or perceived slip will be seized on by the other debaters or the audience. When, in 2015, UKIP's Nathan Gill raised the Conservatives' missed target of reducing net migration to tens of thousands, Stephen Crabb gathered his thoughts in the way he often does in interviews. In a debate setting, however, the pause was taken as confusion by the audience who laughed loudly.*

I won laughter and applause from the audience too when I told Nathan Gill that I would decide when the panelists answered their question. The audience in that debate were more reticent about getting involved than in 2017. Happy to cheer or jeer, the only real interruption came with a shout from one audience member to the politicians to 'give us a referendum.'

FRIDAY 28TH APRIL

ITV Wales' TV debate is causing a few problems.

In previous years, if there'd been questions about who the leaders were in Wales, they'd been resolved within the parties. In 2015 the Conservatives were represented in our debate by the then Welsh Secretary Stephen Crabb and his Labour shadow Owen Smith represented Labour. They were up against two Assembly Members, Leanne Wood and Kirsty Williams; an MEP, Nathan Gill and a non-politician, Pippa Bartolotti. Neither of the MPs raised any objections to non-MPs taking part.

This time around, for Labour, there's no discussion. A Welsh Labour official tells Nick that it'll be the First Minister and not the Shadow Welsh Secretary, who'll take part. 'We'll only be putting Carwyn forward,' they say.

Plaid Cymru and the Liberal Democrats are easy: Leanne Wood and Mark Williams will be their representatives. UKIP don't follow any rules, but despite not being Welsh leader, nobody is challenging the Assembly group leader Neil Hamilton for his place on our stage. As it happens, it looks likely he'll stand in the election too.

It's the Conservatives who are problematic.

As I was told earlier in the week, they're strongly arguing that those taking part in the debates should be politicians who people can vote for in this election, namely candidates to be MPs who can defend manifestos that could at least potentially become UK Government policy. They've already raised with BBC Wales concerns that its first debate, for the Sunday Politics programme, featured no MPs nor parliamentary candidates. We've decided to let the parties make the decision who they want to represent them and the Conservatives have invited Alun Cairns, while making clear that we'd be perfectly happy with Andrew RT Davies.

My suspicion is that there are two ulterior motives behind this: that the Conservatives would prefer the less-experienced Christina Rees to represent Labour and that they don't want Andrew RT Davies to be there for them. There's still tension, I think, over his decision to allow Mark Reckless to join the Welsh Conservative group in the Assembly when he left UKIP.

Meanwhile it seems there are tensions over the sped-up selection process for candidates. Plaid Cymru is facing problems over the Llanelli selection. A popular local hopeful won the most votes at a hustings event, but party bosses ruled him ineligible which meant the business owner who came second is the candidate.

'We've been too nice to local activists in previous elections,' says someone close to the Plaid leadership. 'Leanne's determined to have the best candidates. We're not going to roll over on this one.'

Other parties are experiencing it too. An email arrives from a 'Concerned Bridgend Conservative' saying:

I wanted you to be aware of a situation which is developing. The Party centrally (CCHQ) is trying to impose a shortlist of two candidates on us (Dan Boucher and Karen Robson), neither of whom are from the local area. They had an opportunity to shortlist three candidates but chose not to. This is in spite of high calibre local candidates putting their names forward. This situation has been challenged by a number of members who have written to the Party hierarchy at CCHQ in London and Cardiff to ensure that we have our local choice of candidate on the shortlist. Not only that but the rules simply haven't been followed.

As you will see, instead of reviewing their decision and listening to the local party membership, the Party are closing ranks and bullying us, threatening us with supportive measures if we don't comply and I believe the same is happening in Newport West. The majority of members are up in arms as this is an outrage and tearing our Association apart in a target seat. It is hardly an example of strong and stable leadership in the national interest. This is immoral and treats all of us hard working volunteers who have been here through thick and thin with contempt. Some senior members are threatening to resign and there will be a meeting on Sunday at 7pm at which there will be an attempt to overturn this decision to force a candidate upon us and ensure that our excellent local candidate can contest this important election.

It sounds like the party is causing itself a problem it doesn't need. I call the Conservatives who are already working on a statement. 'I notice it's a Concerned Conservative,' says their press officer. 'Just the one.'

In the middle of this, I'm recording voiceovers for the latest Welsh Bites programmes although they're going to have to wait while the series goes into an enforced election hiatus. One, with former First Minister Rhodri Morgan, clearly causes problems with Ofcom election guidelines. There's a view that the other, with Steps star Ian H. Watkins, is too light-hearted to be broadcast while I'm also covering an election. Given that it includes me responding to his attempts to make me dance along to Steps' songs by saying that, 'I'm a political editor, I don't wiggle,' they may have a point.

"Skin in the Game"

Arguments between broadcasters and political parties about who's allowed on the stage, where they stand on that stage and the order in which they speak are as much part of the drama of TV debates as the soundbites, mistakes and audience interaction.

In Wales in 2017 there was only one party arguing about these things with us as broadcasters and, it seemed, between themselves. From the moment the election was called, the Conservatives insisted that the panel should be made up of parliamentary candidates. From the same moment it was also entirely predictable that Labour and

Plaid Cymru would field AMs in the shape of Carwyn Jones and Leanne Wood.

One senior Conservative thought that we and BBC Wales made a mistake. 'I think the broadcasters should have been much bolder and said, 'We're hosting an election programme, we're discussing a General Election manifesto, we want the Shadow Secretary of State for Wales, we want the Secretary of State for Wales and parliamentary candidate Alun Cairns and the same for UKIP and the same for the Lib Dems and the same for Plaid Cymru, Liz Saville-Roberts or whoever. But it seemed that both ITV and BBC Wales had taken the view that 'we want Carwyn and we want Leanne' and worked back from there.'

I can't speak for the BBC but we hadn't been proscriptive. We'd approached each party and asked them to nominate a representative. In fact we stopped using the term 'Leaders' Debate' for that very reason.

There was never any question about who'd be on stage for Plaid Cymru. It's true that there was a little unease within the party at Leanne Wood's omnipresence in broadcast media during the campaign ('Leanne hogged all the television,' one senior figure told me) and some wished more had been made of Liz Saville Roberts ('a star performer') although maybe they'd forgotten that she wasn't Parliamentary Leader at that point. But there were many more who saw Leanne Wood as their best asset.

'According to opinion polls she's the most popular politician in Wales,' the MP Jonathan Edwards told me, 'so if you don't use her as your asset in an electoral environment, when would you use your leader?'

The campaign team certainly saw her that way. They believed her poll popularity and recognition factor amongst UK media producers made her the best-placed to take part. It also freed up parliamentary candidates to concentrate on 'the ground war.'

It was clear from the start that the leader of the Welsh Liberal Democrats, Mark Williams would represent his party and while Neil Hamilton's official position is UKIP's leader in the Assembly, there was no public disagreement about his taking part because, put simply, the party has no other leader in Wales. As it happens he was also standing as a candidate.

In previous years Labour had fielded Welsh Secretaries or Shadow Welsh Secretaries. It quickly became clear that wouldn't happen this time.

'When the first debate came up,' a member of the campaign team told me, 'there wasn't even a discussion between the Shadow Secretary of State, between our leader, between the campaign team. There was absolute unanimity that Carwyn as Welsh Labour leader would do those debates. It's no exaggeration to say it wasn't a thing because it wasn't a thing. I can't tell you how the conversations went about who would do it because there were no conversations.'

With all this in mind and because we believed that Theresa May's refusal to take part in TV debates might extend to a similar refusal by cabinet members, we'd approached the Welsh Secretary first but made clear we'd be happy with either Tory leader. I was surprised to be told that the Prime Minister's refusal wouldn't prevent Alun Cairns being involved. At the same time I was warned that there would be a problem if the other panelists included non-parliamentary candidates. Internally, top Conservatives used the phrase 'skin in the game' as shorthand for their argument. Those on the stage, they'd say, had to have a skin in the game.

As I record elsewhere, despite making our bid at the beginning of the campaign, we were kept waiting for confirmation until five days before the debate. It was even more stressful for the BBC who'd had Andrew RT Davies confirmed for weeks only to be told he'd been pulled out just over a week before their debate took place. They were told the replacement would be Darren Millar on the Saturday. The debate was taking place on the Tuesday.

Keeping us and the BBC in the dark was, I was told, a deliberate strategy to try to make us change our panel selection. A party source said that 'they believed they could hardball both you and the BBC' to make sure there were no AMs on the stage. 'Hence there was a holding pattern and the plan was to keep things in limbo until the very last moment.' However, that's strongly disputed by others involved in the campaign. To call it a strategy, another source told me, would give it a sense of organisation that simply wasn't there.

Ironically it was the Conservatives who'd originally confused the issue of who takes part in the debates when David Cameron insisted in 2015 that he would only appear if the leaders of Plaid Cymru, the SNP and the Greens were included. That made it difficult for those insisting on a return to parliamentary candidates alone.

'The skin in the game argument didn't work,' said one Tory. 'In 2015 Cameron had Leanne and Sturgeon on the platform because that was a strategy to nullify the left wing vote, to split it. So the precedent was no longer applicable in many ways for what they were trying to achieve.'

SUNDAY 30TH APRIL

On the Sunday Politics programme, Andrew Neil asks Leanne Wood if she'll 'pack it in' as leader if Plaid Cymru doesn't perform well. 'Probably not,' she says. 'I still have work to do.'

There's speculation in the Sunday papers about a post-election reshuffle which reminds me that someone well-placed recently started me thinking about a new role in the future for Alun Cairns. The message is that he's well-regarded by Number 10, has been asked to be 'close' to the manifesto process, specifically on matters related to the Union and was behind a plan for 'something big and transport-related for Wales' to be included. If that's all true I wonder what it could mean for him in any reshuffle. A move or taking on a new job in addition to the Wales portfolio. It's been mentioned to me, significantly, that others, namely Peter Hain, have combined Wales with another cabinet role.

MONDAY 1ST MAY

When I meet a Labour MP, I ask my usual question: 'How's it looking?' The answer is delivered glumly: 'We won't win any new seats. Bridgend's gone. The seats across the North are gone. Albert [Ynys Môn] is gone – sad. Chris Ruane won't win. I hope we keep Newport East.'

I speak to two Conservatives who say, 'Bridgend, yes but we're not counting our chickens.'

A Conservative agent tells me to keep an eye on Cardiff South and Penarth 'as an outlier.' They explain that, 'We have a good candidate who helped in B & R when he stood in Merthyr.[12] We have a very good chance in the Newport seats. The Lib Dems will pour everything into Cardiff Central. Twenty-one [seats] is unlikely, although fourteen or fifteen is possible. But there are six weeks and anything could happen.'

TUESDAY 2ND MAY

We hold a meeting to discuss the debate programme led by Andy, who's producing it.[13] We'll have mini profiles of the audience members asking questions. Four questions on subjects yet to be decided.

In the Wales at Six studio, I'm not the only guest. The other is a twelve-year-old YouTube star called Reuben de Maid. He's in full make-up, shiny suit and sparkling shoes. I look down and my own black Doctor Martens suddenly look very drab.

I'm on to talk about the main focus of the election campaign today which has been Labour's pledge on police officer numbers. From a total for England and Wales of 10,000 the promise includes 853 for Wales. Diane Abbott's confusion over the figures involved in paying for it has turned the attention to the costs of the policy.

The 'Concerned Conservative' from Bridgend gets in touch again:

---

[12] Brecon and Radnorshire
[13] Andy Collinson, Editor of English language current affairs programmes at ITV Cymru Wales

CCHQ has imposed Karen Robson on the Bridgend Conservative Association as expected in spite of the Association's disgust at the attempt to impose a candidate on us. They have rejected our request for them to reconsider the shortlist to include a local candidate and have imposed Ms Robson against the Association's will. Absolute disgrace!

The selection's later confirmed by the Welsh Conservatives. I know Karen Robson and have always found her a decent human being who must hate being the focus of discontent. I guess the grumbles will die down if they win Bridgend.

Jane Dodds is in for Sharp End. I ask her how things are looking for the Lib Dems. She says, 'It's confused. I don't know what's happening in Mont or the other [Lib Dem target seats].'[14]

Adam Price says he thinks Labour in Carmarthen East is imploding.

During the programme itself they argue about Diane Abbott's failure to remember the costs of Labour's policing policy. UKIP's David Rowlands takes a lot of flak over his party's proposed ban on the burqa.

They discuss the leaked account of a dinner between Theresa May and Jean-Claude Juncker. Adam Price describes it as, 'International diplomacy conducted in the spirit of Basil and Sybil Fawlty.'

---

[14] Montgomeryshire

WEDNESDAY 3RD MAY

Phew! I receive a letter from the courts service telling me that my jury service has been deferred until next year. I'm not quite sure what would have happened otherwise because the date when I was required by law to present myself was election week itself.

While Parliament is being dissolved and Theresa May is accusing EU politicians and officials of interfering in the election campaign, I'm taking part in an ITV Current Affairs forum. It coincides with the announcement of our election coverage, including the network debate. ITV's editor of regional news, Guy Phillips tells me that what I hear is right, that they believe Theresa May is 'resolute' about refusing to take part but there's less certainty about Jeremy Corbyn's position. If he continues to refuse to take part, Guy says the plan is to empty-chair both. The debate will be shortened and there'll be 'spin room' interviews with senior Labour and Conservative politicians. But there's a feeling that ITV must stand firm, that the Leaders' Debate is just that and only leaders take part not stand-ins.

That reminds me that the Conservative problem for our own debate is still unresolved. I hear BBC Wales are experiencing the same difficulties: the Tories are insisting that Alun Cairns will only take part if he faces Christina Rees not Carwyn Jones. Labour won't countenance putting anyone other than Carwyn Jones forward. It needs to be resolved. Our debate takes place two weeks today.

A reply to my e-moan arrives from the Conservative party: 'Apologies for such a late response to your email. Our intention was never to intend any slight to ITV Wales, but I do appreciate your point re questions. We will definitely be back on a political visit to Wales soon and I will make sure we bear these points in mind.'

I reply with a request for not just a question at the next event, but an interview.

THURSDAY 4TH MAY/FRIDAY 5TH MAY

I cast my votes and then take the dog for a walk to Beechwood Park. I notice that the listed Beechwood House which is at the centre of the park and so imposing in my childhood memories, is a polling station. Surely it must be one of the most elegant.

22.00 A downbeat statement comes from Welsh Labour. Christina Rees praises Labour workers for their efforts, adding that, 'It always inspires me that even when times seem tough for Labour, they never fail to rise to the challenge with a passion and energy that no other party can match. Our Welsh Labour councils and councillors have a huge amount to be proud of and whatever the results tonight they will all continue to play a crucial role in working with the Welsh Labour Government to deliver for their communities and stop the Tories walking all over Wales.'

23.00 The Conservatives are making it clear that these council elections are part of their overall General election campaign. The party sends us a statement saying, 'We are out there to win. These are Theresa May's candidates – it is all part of a strong and stable leadership, a Conservative prime minister that is out fighting for the country and the council candidates are her candidates.'

Nick and a handful of others stay in the office overnight. After a few hours' sleep I go back just before 4am when the picture is becoming clear. Labour's having a difficult night as expected in some councils but is holding on in others, which will encourage it and concern the other parties. It's kept Newport, where the Conservatives have high hopes of making gains in June. It's lost Blaenau Gwent to Independents. The Labour leader of Merthyr Tydfil has lost his seat and it's tied between Labour and Independents although the final result won't be known for a month.[15] The Conservatives look likely to win control of Monmouthshire which they've run in coalition with the Lib Dems.

A Welsh Labour source assesses the story so far:

Fantastic night in Flintshire, with Labour gaining three seats and retaining control... The picture in Wrexham is far more nuanced than top lines suggest. Makes read-across to Ian Lucas at GE very tricky. We are still ahead of the Tories in a seat they are targeting.

Context on the situation in Merthyr Tydfil & Blaenau Gwent. Both were 2012 gains – both were Independent controlled prior to that. There is a long history of Independent support on both councils, making any read-across to GE results broadly meaningless..

---

[15] A month later, Labour picked up enough seats in the final ward to win a majority.

04.30 Labour's held onto Neath Port Talbot although Plaid Cymru has surprised many by making some gains there.

A Plaid Cymru source says, 'It looks very positive for us at the moment. Story seems to be Plaid and Tory gains vs Labour and UKIP losses.

'Particularly positive to see us breaking new ground in places like Bridgend, Aberavon and Blaenau Gwent. We've also made gains in Wrexham and Neath.

'Also seems like our vote is holding up well in Ceredigion despite running the council there, implementing the cuts from Welsh Government, so we're pleased at the moment, particularly given our strongholds are yet to come tomorrow.'

04.50 The final result is in for Ceredigion: no overall control.

05.00 Monmouthshire is a Conservative gain. It's been run for the last five years as a Tory-Lib Dem coalition. Even with the disappointment, the always-optimistic Lib Dems still see signs here that the strategy of targeting ultra-Remainers might work though. A source tells me, 'The Constituency voted Remain – we took seats from Tories. We haven't seen the fall in support that Labour has seen elsewhere.'

05.30 Labour's lost Bridgend to no overall control. The council boundary isn't the same as that of the parliamentary constituency, but that loss is symbolic. After all Bridgend is the First Minister's constituency.

A Liberal Democrat source tells me, 'It doesn't look as though our vote has held up in parts of Cardiff. Tories who previously voted for us have decided to vote Tory again. We've made some gains in Ceredigion. Our vote hasn't held up as we were expecting to in Swansea. We've been hit by the General Election factor which has changed the tone of debate. We're squeezed from both sides as people see it as a Conservative-Labour decision and are looking away from liberal issues. In terms of party organisation, the election's a year too early for us. We haven't had the breathing space to rebuild [after Assembly election] that the party in England has.'

I relocate to a spot in front of the Senedd in Cardiff Bay which is where I'll be for the next few hours. I'll be giving live updates to the Good Morning Britain programme on the situation here in Wales.

06.50 Labour not only holds onto Swansea but increases its majority by one.

07.00 A new statement arrives from Shadow Welsh Secretary Christina Rees. Although she refers to the 'difficult night' in Blaenau Gwent and Merthyr Tydfil and the 'blow' of losing councillors, it's more positive than that which she made nine hours ago.

The Welsh Conservatives are upbeat too: 'We have seen some encouraging results overnight – notably winning control of Monmouthshire County Council – but we take nothing for granted. It's too early to give an accurate picture, and we can't assume council results will be repeated at the General Election.'

08.20 It's confirmed that Labour has held Cardiff despite the infighting that has become so public.

Carwyn Jones tweets – 'A testing night for many of our candidates. Thanks to all for standing and for your hard work. There will be better times.'

By the time all the results are in, the picture is clear. Labour's lost some symbolic councils but has survived. It kept hold of Cardiff despite predictions that it would lose it and remained in control in Newport, a top Tory target. It increased its majority in Swansea, kept the same number of seats it previously had in Wrexham and Flintshire and remained in control of Rhondda Cynon Taf and Neath Port Talbot. The Conservatives have failed to make as many gains as expected, but they have grounds for optimism for June 8th. They are now in control in Monmouthshire and are the largest party in Denbighshire and the Vale of Glamorgan.

Plaid Cymru points out that it's come within four seats of its best ever number of council seats. It's retained control in Gwynedd and is the largest party still in Ceredigion. UKIP has no councillors.

Andrew RT Davies says, 'We are emboldened by the results,' but adds that, 'there is also still a general election to fight … Our work is far from done and we are steeling ourselves for the challenge ahead.'

The Lib Dems have lost a further eleven councillors but Welsh leader Mark Williams sees hope: 'We have gained seats from Labour in Monmouth and Neath Port Talbot, seats from the Conservatives in Flintshire, and from Plaid Cymru in Ceredigion.'

A very senior Labour person tells me, 'Bridgend is going to be very difficult now. Wrexham too. The Newports are more positive, Gower too but we're not there. We'll still have the most seats after the election.'

A Labour person messages me on twitter: 'Nothing in these results makes me think Labour will do any better than polls suggesting. Only crumbs of comfort are Lib Dems and Plaid going nowhere so Jo Stevens should cling on in Cardiff Central. And unlikely to see any Nat breakthrough in valleys heartlands. But truth is where Tories are competing they are winning.'

A third, less depressed Labour source tells me, 'The reality is we're in the middle of a pendulum swing. But it was a far smaller Tory swing than everyone expected so our results were patchy but not a write off.'

I go to Bridgend to interview the First Minister. When I get to Carwyn Jones' house, my cameraman Gareth is playing the family's piano. The First Minister is in jeans and an untucked shirt in a kitchen full of fizzy drinks and crisps for his daughter's party tonight.

He tries to put the loss of Bridgend into context: 'Actually in the time I've been AM for Bridgend, only on two occasions did we have an overall majority in Bridgend. It's quite normal for Bridgend [council] to have no party in overall control. We had a worse result in 2004 actually than now.'

But, I ask, surely you're not relaxed about losing it?

'Absolutely not. We lost some very good councillors last night and we are close to control of the council, by far the biggest party and we'll bounce back as we have done before. For me, I was being told before the election, you're going to lose the big cities, you're going to be wiped out across most of your own constituency. It hasn't happened that way and to my mind, a lot of people were hesitating about voting Conservative because they knew what had happened under Conservative governments in the past and now.'

I ask if Jeremy Corbyn should consider his position.

'I've said before we have a mountain to climb and its hugely important that Jeremy works hard now to convince people that he is a good candidate for Prime Minister. He's convinced the party and he'll know that work needs to be done over the next few weeks.'

On air I say that our poll last week showed that Labour would scrape through and it has. It may have suffered a loss of some symbolic local authorities but it has survived this particular test here in Wales.

But I say that the Conservatives will be pleased that they're winning in the kind of places that they need to, to make a difference in Wales. Bridgend, I remark, is a microcosm of the titanic struggle that's happening in this election.

"Agreement... for the time being"

The long wait for confirmation on who would be the Conservative in our debate led us to think that a power struggle was going on between

Alun Cairns and Andrew RT Davies. In fact the two men reached agreement quickly even if it later broke down spectacularly.

Broadly they agreed that it seemed unlikely that the broadcasters would back down over the involvement of non-candidates in the debates and so Davies would be the Tory representative in all three programmes. These were our Election Debate and two BBC programmes: its Leaders' Debate with Huw Edwards and a half-hour 'Ask the Leader' involving single politicians taking questions from a live audience.

Memories of the agreement differ between the two camps. The Davies team were certain that 'the debates should be done by the same person, ideally Alun but Andrew will do it on the basis that he does them all.'

The Cairns team said, 'We had agreed that if it was debating other Assembly members it would be Andrew; if you're debating an audience to talk about reserved matters in the manifesto it would be Alun and there was no reason why it has to be one person doing all three. No reason why it couldn't be both.'

Before the election was called, Davies had booked an overseas holiday with his family to celebrate a milestone wedding anniversary. When it was agreed that he should do the debates he bought extra tickets which meant he could return from the holiday, take part in the Ask the Leader programme and the BBC Wales debate, then rejoin his family. His team told me they were going to drive him back from the BBC debate to Luton airport so that he could catch an early hours flight.

This agreement and these complicated plans meant that we were *told on Friday 12th May that Davies would be taking part in our debate despite the party's reservations about the decision.*

At least though the two leaders were content with that arrangement. For the time being.

MONDAY 8TH MAY

A meeting with top Plaid Cymru people. They tell us that based on analysis of the council results Plaid could win seven Westminster seats: the three it holds now: Arfon, Carmarthen East and Dinefwr and Dwyfor Meirionnydd along with Caerphilly, Ceredigion, Rhondda and Ynys Môn. Using another model it could add Cardiff West. 'We were also close in Neath and Llanelli,' they say.

One of those present adds Blaenau Gwent into the mix, saying, 'We were well advised not to challenge the independents in the council election, they are coming behind us increasingly.' They claim former independent MP Dai Davies is on the Plaid candidate's leaflets.[16]

The prospect of Plaid Cymru winning between seven and ten seats seems unlikely but this senior figure is convinced that the Labour vote is up for grabs. 'The result at a UK level is a foregone conclusion,' they say. 'But the results are very unpredictable in terms of constituencies. There are loads of wildcard seats, anything can happen.'

----
[16] Later confirmed Dai Davies told Saul Cooke-Black of the South Wales Argu that 'It is about the person not the party. Nigel [Cobner, the Plaid Cymru candidate] is a local man who cares about the local people.'

Plaid will run the campaign as 'a collection of simultaneous by-elections rather than a General Election. Local factors will be critical in success or failure. Obviously there'll be a national campaign and message – 'defending Wales' which has become the 'forgotten country' – but the path to victory is different in different seats.'

The party is 'investing heavily' in what will be a 'well-resourced' election because it thinks it's a 'fantastic opportunity' to get its 'best ever tally of MPs'.

At half past three I tweet, 'It is happening again. @roger_scully has arrived at @ITVWales HQ #ScullyWatch17' That's because Roger is with us to talk through our second poll of the campaign.

ScullyWatch is the light-hearted social media monitoring of his appearances. He's certainly become the go-to person on Welsh polling. As well as us, he's regularly on Sky News, BBC Wales and network as well as other UK and international TV networks. I think he's quite enjoying his high media profile.

As for the poll, it shows the Conservatives still ahead with an extraordinary 41% vote share. But Labour is fighting back and how: up five points to 35%. All the others are down: Plaid Cymru to 11%, the Lib Dems to 7% and UKIP to 4%.

It shows a possible reason why the Conservatives are still ahead. Brexit is still the number one issue and voters trust the Conservatives on it. Carwyn Jones may be more popular than Theresa May but the Conservatives are more trusted than Labour or any other party when it comes to Brexit.

Roger says a Welsh Government adviser told him the first poll was a blessing in disguise, a kick up the backside for their supporters, but that they're still worried about 'another four and a half weeks of May v. Corbyn.'

I wonder if there's evidence for Labour voters making the journey to voting Conservative via voting for UKIP and then Leave. By way of an answer, he says that the Conservatives are still doing very well among UKIP and Leave voters and a good proportion of those were Labour. The amount of Labour voters likely to vote Tory has to be 'non-trivial'. But it depends where those switchers are. If it's in the Valleys, a swing to the Tories is not so much use to them.

He's been in a twitter row with Carl Sargeant on the one hand and Adam Price on the other. He thinks that Plaid is overstating its claim of an 'historic breakthrough' in the council elections. The poll shows the party is making some ground but not seeing any kind of surge.

On another matter, he highlights the incredibly low popularity rating for Neil Hamilton. He's never seen a leader rating as low, ever, so he's been checking with fellow psephologists and none of them have seen one as low either.

Roger's online article begins: 'Labour is fighting back in Wales –but the Conservatives are still on course for an historic triumph at the general election.'

In an interview with me he says, 'This poll shows us the last poll was not a fluke, the Conservatives really are doing that well in Wales. What's different about this poll is that the Labour party have made some ground back. It tells us something about where we are in Welsh politics that the Labour party might be relieved to be only six percentage points behind the Conservatives, four and a half weeks from a General Election.'

Welsh Labour meanwhile launches its campaign in Cardiff with no mention of Jeremy Corbyn. It publishes its five main election pledges, three of which are to do with devolved areas, and as such, not anything that will be affected by this election.[17]

---

[17] Protecting the NHS and social care budgets, keeping free school breakfasts and investing more in school standards and providing twenty thousand more affordable homes in Wales.

Carwyn Jones tells Owain, 'It's a Welsh Labour launch and Welsh Labour pledges. There'll be a G.B. launch over the next few days and that's what Jeremy will front up.'

In the studio I say that devolution can be confusing at the best of times but party politics at the moment is using devolved areas for political reasons that are confusing us even more. This is nothing new of course. In 2015 the Conservatives made the Welsh Health Service a major part of its campaign. It seems this year all parties have learned from that approach.

Someone close to Carwyn Jones tells us that the First Minister will take part in the debates but 'they don't want it out there yet because it will be a story.' This is because of the party's previous insistence that Labour's representative at General Election time should be Secretary of State or Shadow Secretary of State rather than the Welsh leader.[18]

On Sharp End, the Conservative MP Craig Williams is cautious about the poll: 'I'm encouraged but we don't believe polls when we're doing badly and I don't believe it now. I'm encouraged by the mood music but we mustn't be complacent. Labour are a real threat and can turn their vote out.'

Plaid Cymru's Steffan Lewis repeats what I was told earlier: 'What we're going to see is forty concurrent by-elections and I think that

---

[18] As it happens, there's virtually no comment on Labour's new approach because all the attention is on the Conservative confusion.

whilst there'll be national mood music, that'll impact definitely. The exceptional nature of this election means that absolutely anything can happen. Everything's in play. A number of people who used to put their faith in Labour are looking for a new political home.'

UKIP's Gareth Bennett never toes any party line, not even his own. 'Strange,' he says. 'Brexit was traditionally our issue, now people are seemingly looking to the Conservatives because they are a party of government.'

The Lib Dem peer Jenny Randerson insists her party is still in contention: 'In our target constituencies, we are in play.'

Labour's Hannah Blythyn is not counting her chickens: 'It's not an ideal situation to be in. As someone once said, things can only get better.'

I put Neil Hamilton's low leadership ratings to Gareth Bennett and he says this: 'That sounds not brilliant. Room for improvement. I'll tell him tomorrow.'

TUESDAY 9TH MAY

Owain has heard that UKIP's former Welsh leader, Nathan Gill, could be about to defect to the Conservatives. His source tells him that Gill has removed UKIP colours from his website and that Paul Nuttall has told the source that Gill has had a massive row with UKIP's treasurer. A quick check of the website reveals no mention of UKIP on the home page, certainly no party colours but I don't know what it looked like before. Owain texts Gill asking him if he's about to join the Conservatives, to which Gill replies, 'No.'

A Conservative AM texts to say, 'I've not heard [about Nathan Gill] but he [Andrew RT Davies] is a law unto himself when it comes to the Conservative/Independent group.'

In Cardiff Bay I bump into a senior Labour politician who's just about to go canvassing and who says, 'It's looking scary.'

'How bad?' I ask. 'As bad as our poll?'

'At least as bad,' is the response. 'And then what happens after that?'

Apparently, people answering canvassers say they differentiated between last week's local elections and the General Election. They may have voted Labour at a local level but won't for Westminster.

WEDNESDAY 10TH MAY

More chatter about the debates with two BBC reporters and a Conservative official who says, 'Andrew is raring to go.' They're not quite sure why they [those around Alun Cairns] have made such an issue of it. 'Is it the height thing?' they muse.

There's strong speculation that the Welsh Tories will return to the question of his leadership after the election. Owain is told by a senior AM not given to gossip that, 'Andrew's in real trouble' and that Jonathan Evans, the Welsh Conservative chair, is livid.

I have another email from the UK Conservative Party's press office: 'Again apologies for the tardy response. We will certainly look to try and get an interview in on our next trip to Wales. I'm looping in Tom, who is Head of Broadcast for the campaign, so he's aware.'

THURSDAY 11TH MAY

Labour's draft manifesto has been leaked and it's making quite a splash with its plans to end austerity and renationalise some industries. But Welsh Labour doesn't want any part of it. An official statement arrives:

*Reports of leaked manifestos relate to an old, draft version of a UK document. 'It is **not** Welsh Labour's manifesto and contains many England-only proposals. Welsh Labour will be publishing its own distinct manifesto, building on the success of our five pledges for Wales.*

It may have been an old draft but the final draft is being agreed today.

At Labour's conference in 2016, after a lot of shouting, briefing and counter-briefing, Welsh Labour won a lot more power over the way it organises itself. It also won a bigger say in the party's internal workings. This includes the right for the Welsh Leader to attend the joint meeting of the Shadow Cabinet and National Executive, known as the Clause V meeting. It is these bodies that agree the Westminster election manifesto.

For the first time, Carwyn Jones has taken up that right and is filmed arriving at the meeting in London and being asked if he were responsible for the leak of the draft manifesto. It's nothing personal, reporters are asking everyone who arrives.

In an official statement, Carwyn Jones is quoted as saying, 'Crucially, strong bonds with our Labour colleagues has meant that Wales's voice has also been heard loud and clear in the UK manifesto.'

Tim Farron arrives in Cardiff to help the Liberal Democrats launch their Welsh campaign. Conveniently for us, it's right outside our offices in Cardiff Bay. Farron warns that, 'If the Tories get a landslide, Wales will be taken for granted.'

Vince tells me that he has begged Andrew RT Davies to cut down on the campaign visits to McDonald's because he's worried about his own health. Being on the road campaigning means they often end up having McDonald's for breakfast and lunch. Vince tells me that last year all the fast food started affecting his mood. It sounds like the Welsh Tories are re-enacting Morgan Spurlock's *Super Size Me*. I suspect the other parties could tell similar stories.

FRIDAY 12TH MAY

The NHS in England is under cyber attack. I ask the Welsh Government what the situation is in Wales and am told, 'We have had no reported cyber incidents affecting NHS Wales but are monitoring the situation closely.'

Nick gets a call from the Conservatives. It'll be Andrew RT Davies not Alun Cairns taking part in our debate.

Boris Johnson is in Newport. It's a sign of how seriously the Conservatives are taking Newport West and think they're still in with a chance of winning Newport East.

Predictably, it turns into a circus with the TV footage showing hordes of journalists, cameras and others crammed into Newport market. It's chaos. Notorious for being pro-cake and pro-having it, he's served teacake in one of the market cafes. At a craft stall, he paints some concrete letters spelling out his name, using blue paint of course. My colleague Megan asks the stallholder if he answered any of her questions about policies.[19] She says, 'No details, he was too busy painting.'

Megan tries to get some details from him on the kind of trade deals Welsh farmers can expect. The Foreign Secretary tells her he has, 'absolutely no doubt that we can get a fantastic deal for Welsh farmers.' Megan asks if that involves tariffs. 'There's absolutely no reason why you would have tariffs.'

Another big hitter, Labour's Tom Watson, is also here. Actually, he's visiting ten different seats across the South. He's asked why Welsh Labour is emphasising Carwyn Jones rather than Jeremy Corbyn. 'We've got a very strong First Minister, we've got a track record that we're all proud of and is shaping the direction and destiny of this country so why wouldn't you focus on the First Minister when you've got a devolved settlement?'

I receive a call from a Conservative asking why Andrew RT Davies is representing the party in our debate, not Alun Cairns. When I explain, they say, 'He [Davies] is totally the wrong person for it and it looks like he [Cairns] has bottled it. I'm going to push back against it.'

SUNDAY 14TH MAY

I talk to Branwen Cennard, the TV writer and producer whom I know from talking to her as she developed S4C's racy political

---

[19] Megan Boot, ITV Wales Education reporter who was given the task of covering the Conservatives for the duration of the campaign.

drama *Byw Celwydd*. It's often filmed in parts of the Senedd during Assembly down-time.

When Theresa May visited just days after becoming Prime Minister, she was being welcomed by the First Minister in the main entrance of the Senedd while in the Cwrt below, fictional politics was being acted out. I only discovered this when I accidentally pressed the wrong button on the glass-sided lift which deposited me slap behind one of the stars, Ffion Dafis, who was in the middle of a scene.

Branwen is Plaid's candidate in the Rhondda. She tells me she hadn't planned to put herself forward but had seen on the news that Leanne Wood was considering standing against Chris Bryant. Branwen thought that might mean a by-election for the Assembly seat and for the first time ever she may have put her name forward. She went away on holiday and forgot all about it until the Plaid leader rang her out of the blue to say that she'd decided not to stand for Westminster and that they were therefore looking for a candidate. I ask her how real politics compares to her fiction and she says, 'It's like *Byw Celwydd* times twenty-five.'

'Forces Beyond Our Control'

In much the same way that Plaid Cymru found itself squeezed out of the election campaign by the two big parties, so its own campaign has escaped much of the post-election scrutiny devoted to Labour and the Conservatives. And there are those who think that that's all the post mortem needed. 'There was a sense of helplessness, that we were affected by forces beyond our control,' said a senior member of the campaign team. There were no complaints about candidates, canvassers or those who fought the 'air war'. There were no gaffes, discipline held, message delivery was good. But after a while those messages just weren't breaking through.

Canvassers reported positive responses on the ground for most of the campaign. There was every sense that Ynys Môn was within reach for the party and there were good signs in Labour heartland areas Llanelli, Rhondda and Blaenau Gwent. But the big shift towards Labour wasn't always detected and when it was, Plaid didn't seem to have the flexibility to react. One veteran told me they expected Hywel [Williams] to come back with a majority of three thousand. In the end it was just ninety-two votes.

The MP Jonathan Edwards described it to me:

'There was nothing coming from our opponents on the ground and I didn't feel anything in the air. I thought it was going to be a very comfortable victory until two days before the election and then you just had a feeling something was happening. You just noticed. Hold on something's not quite right and then it was just re-emergence of the Labour vote it came from nowhere.

Absolutely nothing on the ground. Alarm bells sounded maybe a week before the election when we found there were huge numbers of last minute registered voters that we had never seen before who'd suddenly appeared. I think what Labour had done was identify people who weren't on the register, identified them on whatever data systems they use and they got them on the electoral roll and that was the big difference.'

Identifying voters was a problem. Echoing similar complaints that I report from Conservatives to the use of what they pejoratively call 'American' canvassing techniques used to identify and target likely voters, one senior figure said to me, 'You're going down roads and you're walking past houses and people look through the window and see a candidate walking past. That's a crazy way of doing it.'

Worse than that, it meant that the party didn't reach out to those people who'd never voted or stopped voting, people who may well have been open to considering Plaid.

'We let a whole load of people be outside the focus of our campaign,' I was told. 'People who'd been ignored, who felt they were outside the system and that nobody gave a damn about them, the very people that we ought to be getting in ... we didn't do this.'

Members of the campaign team acknowledge that data capture methods weren't up to scratch. 'We didn't have enough information on the ground. There were red flags in Ynys Môn and Arfon such as increased voter registrations but we had a lack of intelligence and weren't able to adapt effectively.'

One possible way of adapting could have been in its choice of candidates. Plaid's ray of hope was Ben Lake who at the age of just twenty-four won the party a fourth seat. Plaid veterans smile when they talk about him being the ideal candidate: young, bright, enthusiastic and local. Perhaps unfairly some contrast choosing him with the choice of candidate for Ynys Môn, the party's former leader, former MP and former AM, Ieuan Wyn Jones.

At the time of selection though it was seen as a canny move. Politics is different on Anglesey and long, local links are highly valued. But some within Plaid identify a tendency to 'look back at past heroes with rose-tinted glasses, thinking they're the future. The pressure is always there. Someone is always saying let's bring Dafydd Wigley back, let's bring Elfyn Llwyd back. We need to look to the future.'

There have been other criticisms of campaign decisions. Before he was suspended from the Plaid Assembly group, Neil McEvoy said the party seemed irrelevant to young people and had hamstrung itself by co-operating with Labour in the Assembly. I've also heard complaints that the campaign failed to attack Labour at a UK level over its divided Brexit divisions. It was seen as a perfect opportunity to drive a wedge between Labour in Wales and Labour in London but whether from a wish not to alienate Leave voters in the Valleys or to antagonise Labour in the Assembly, some feel that the attack wasn't made strongly enough. One even wondered out loud to me whether it was because privately 'Leanne is as unsafe on Europe as Corbyn.'

When I spoke to Jonathan Edwards he was optimistic about what had been achieved in a polarised campaign. 'At the end of the day forget about vote share or whatever, it's about seats and we came out of that election with four seats. Now two of them are marginal seats but we've got four seats, it's our joint best ever result and that's with a Conservative government in London. It's far more favourable en-vironment for us to fight a Westminster election when it's a Labour UK Government and we pick up those protest votes. So it's very difficult to be hyper-critical about the election.'

MONDAY 15TH MAY

I spend most of the day preparing for the debate. I've been researching in every spare moment in and out of the office for a couple of weeks now. Based on my experience of preparing for the previous two, what I aim for is to read all the manifestos, research other policy pledges made during the campaign along with earlier, sometimes contradictory positions, and list some challenges for each of the participants. I try to note likely standpoints, slogans, attacks and have some essential facts and figures. On the night I'll have a mixture of scripts on cards, challenges and possible questions on ipad and facts and figures on paper. It's still not enough because the debate amongst five or six very confident, very robust people moves very quickly.

This time around few of the manifestos have been published so I'm largely reliant on previous documents and any public statements or pledges made so far. It's a lot of information to find and remember so I've organised my research into two big iCloud documents.

One, 'Facts and figures' is exactly what you'd expect. It contains twelve pages of bullet points listing where the parties stand on Brexit and related issues. It's far too much but I'd rather know that the information is there. I'll print it and paste it onto cue cards so that I have it at my fingertips.

The other document is fourteen pages entitled, 'Challenges' and I'll keep this open on my iPad on my lectern so that I can whizz back and forth through it. I've organised potential challenges and criticisms for each of the leaders, based on what I know of their likely positions, and I've arranged it in order of the questions that we plan to take on the evening. I'll barely use a fraction of it but I like to go into it knowing that I have as much information and am primed for as many potential challenges as possible.

The cue cards arrive in the office, a large pack of A5-sized cards with the programme's title on the front. They somehow make it all more real.

Elsewhere Leanne Wood has told the BBC's Victoria Derbyshire that she used cannabis when she was 'younger and a student.' She was asked too about the idea of 'boy jobs and girl jobs' as mentioned by Theresa May. She said her partner does all the housework 'so all the jobs are his really.'

That reminds me of last year when we recorded a Bites programme with her. She's protective of her family so we arranged to film the programme in a cafe near where she lives. She was quite open about not being a very good cook because her partner does all the cooking at home.

We were to make omelettes which should have been simple, but we both demonstrated our failings as chefs when most of her omelette mixture spilled out of the griddle and turned into a burned, sticky mess. In our defence, nobody told us the griddle was lacking an important part that would have avoided disaster.

She laughed about it on the programme and told me other people poked fun of her too. One woman told her she liked her and would be voting for her but never to invite her round to dinner. I joked that it was the omelette that won her the Rhondda.

On Sharp End this evening, the Conservative Dan Boucher is opposed by all the other guests over cyber security. He insists it's not a question of funding, saying that the government is funding cyber security. The other four are certain that it is a question of money. They think the Welsh NHS has been lucky to escape it although Labour's Jo Stevens says it wasn't luck, it was forward thinking by the Welsh Government.

Too Much Leanne?

There's no doubting the relief expressed by Plaid Cymru at winning Ceredigion. In the hours before it, things had looked very bleak for the party. Naturally that raised questions about Leanne Wood's continued leadership. She was on the point of resigning before Ceredigion, a senior Plaid person told me long after the election. She'd prepared a resignation statement, said another.

In fact she was asleep when the result came in. Her team were by then confident of Ceredigion and knew she'd need to leave early in the morning to go there.

It was true that she was prepared to resign if Plaid had lost seats and that if there'd been no gains, she would have thought seriously about it. In that event there would have been a holding statement with a view to making a full statement a few days later. In the end there was no pressure on her that day, apart from a familiar problem complained of by many in Plaid, that of not celebrating success and dwelling on negatives.

One party figure talks admiringly of Wood's 'stamina and deter-mination' during the whole campaign when she was the public face, on TV and radio in Wales and at a network level seemingly every day at the same time as carrying out a punishing regime of campaign visits. She also refused to 'hide' when a row broke out over selection in Llanelli, instead confronting critics in a hostile meeting.

Some wondered if there was 'too much Leanne' as I've reported elsewhere. But supporters say that her visible presence freed up can-didates to fight the ground war. That was a deliberate policy, using the leader and 'key communicators' such as Rhun ap Iorwerth and Adam Price to make the case in the media, leaving others free to campaign face to face.

There were other grumbles though. Some criticised the public decision-making over whether or not to stand in the Rhondda. 'She could have won it, or at least made a damned good showing,' a senior figure told me.

She was certainly under intense pressure internally to stand. 'Most of it was well-intentioned,' an ally of hers told me. 'But some deliber-ately wanted to put her in a position where she couldn't be party leader any more.' In any case they don't think 'in her heart of hearts' she ever would have stood. 'She's incredibly principled; it's essential for her not to go against values she's stated and she's always said the Assembly and Wales are where her priorities are, not going to Westminster. Maybe she would have won, but in the long term it would have been damaging to her.'

And there are those who see her leadership as having stalled for some time. 'We're in the doldrums,' a senior figure told me. There are

*rumblings about too much time getting involved in twitter spats –
'some fairly stupid tweets,' as it was put to me – along with 'dissatisfaction' with a 'dysfunctional' Assembly group and an apparent failure
to build on momentum that she established in the run-up to the
2015 General Election. Even her dramatic victory in the Rhondda
in 2016 has been described by another source as being a false indica-
tion of progress. They compared it to the 'slip coaches' of an earlier
railway age, which were brought into station by a momentum that
was already reducing.*

*At the time of writing, Leanne Wood remains leader; there's no
immediate sign of a leadership challenge and constitutionally she
doesn't need to face one until 2018. Since the election, however, she's
received plenty of advice to bring any dissatisfaction to a head and
call a John Major-style 'back me or sack me' leadership election that
could see her time in charge last until the next Assembly election in
2021 or come to an early end. Once again, Plaid Cymru is at a crossroads.*

TUESDAY 16TH MAY

The Conservatives spring a surprise announcement: a pledge to
abolish the Severn tolls. The press release which arrives without
warning is very revealing in its emphasis on the Prime Minister.
It's headed: 'Theresa May: I will abolish tolls on Severn Crossings
between Wales and England.' It goes on to say that, 'Theresa May
today pledges to abolish' the tolls and that, if elected, 'Theresa
May's Conservatives will scrap the tolls'.

There's a quote from Alun Cairns saying that, 'Theresa May

will ensure that economic prosperity is spread across the United Kingdom.' However, when a member of our newsdesk approaches his team to arrange a clip, they're told he can't say anything until Theresa May has announced it.

Plaid Cymru launches what it's not calling its manifesto but instead calling its 'Action Plan to protect, preserve and promote' Wales. It includes promises to ensure that Wales doesn't lose out after Brexit. As well as promising to protect the rights of EU citizens already living here, scrapping the 'bedroom tax' and increasing the top rate of income tax. Leanne Wood tells my colleague James that her party accepts the referendum result but wants to get the best deal for Wales.[20]

Talking of Plaid, some colleagues arrive from the Tonight programme team. They're putting together a programme on Leanne Wood as part of our network coverage. I'm to be the pundit so I've been doing some swotting on her life and views. I also watch online the Face to Face programme I did with her back in 2012.

I find the interview really strange, as if I'm taking part in Mastermind with Leanne Wood as my specialist subject.

I join Andy and some of the debate team on a visit to Stanwell School in Penarth where it'll happen tomorrow. Stanwell is a school with a good reputation but I'm not sure what to expect of its theatre. If anything, I have in mind a sports hall with perhaps removable seating. We're led through our OB trucks into a

---

[20] James Crichton-Smith who was the embedded reporter with Plaid Cymru during the campaign.

backstage area, through black curtains and into what astonishingly is a fully-fledged theatre with a great stage, acoustics and rows of (permanent) seats. It's really impressive.

I'm introduced to the set designer who's keeping an eye on the preparations. It's all had to be designed and produced with very little time but already looks good. The panels behind us are nearly in place. The lecterns are positioned but without the colours and lighting. Large lights which will be above us are still on the floor of the stage. There's timber, cables and plastic lying all over the place. The cameras are in place though so I can get a good idea of where I'll need to stand and look. I have a position at the edge of the stage for the opening of each part and then for the debate I'm almost in the middle of the other lecterns.

It's all very impressive and exciting. We just have to do it now.

Playing Politicians

Rehearsals are good fun. In 2015 I had to pretend to be Leanne Wood twice, one in ITV's Southbank HQ and one in the cavernous studio in Salford, normally used for 'The Voice'. I prepared myself by reading the manifesto and committing to memory as many slogans as possible. I found it surprisingly, even scarily, easy to remember slogans.

In that rehearsal Peter McMahon, the Political Editor at ITV Border, took the role of Nicola Sturgeon. We tried to mimic the way we thought the two leaders would work together to give Julie Etchingham an idea of what to expect. At the end of the debate we also hugged as, it turned out, did the real Sturgeon and Wood.

In 2016 I had to pretend to be Amber Rudd for an EU referendum debate rehearsal. I read some speeches and articles and watched a few interviews she'd given, noting down the sort of slogans she'd used. It's surprising and a little scary how quickly I adopted the rhythms, words and phrases used by the politicians. I failed to guess how acidic she'd be in the real thing about her fellow Tory Boris Johnson.

The parties have their own and I've heard of politicians and advisers enjoying the rare chance to have a go at their boss. I was disappointed to learn there were rehearsals of lines in 2017 but no role-playing.

WEDNESDAY 17TH MAY

Stanwell School's theatre is a hive of activity when I arrive at lunchtime. It's looking good: everything's in place and everything seems to be ready.

Our rehearsal comes mid-afternoon and this is where we'll spot any likely problems. My colleagues are taking the roles of the leaders. Rob Osborne is Neil Hamilton, Tom Anderton is Carwyn Jones, James Crichton-Smith is Leanne Wood and Sion Jenkins is Mark Williams.

As an ex-pupil, Megan Boot, who's standing in for Andrew RT Davies, is no stranger to this stage. She's played many roles before this, her biggest being Eponine in *Les Miserables*. There's no misery from this lot. They throw themselves into character, attacking each other, trotting out all the slogans that we've been given as sound bites for weeks, interrupting each other, shouting, causing me problems by going over time and breaching guidelines, although that's mainly Rob.

We run through a few sections of the programmes for my sake and for Fiona the director and the gallery team. It's fair to say it's going well. Doing three of these debates in as many years has given us a level of expertise which is on show even during this rehearsal.

I take a break and go to get showered and changed. I stop off to buy some sandwiches for the end of the night. I know I won't be able to eat beforehand because I'll be so uneasy. When I come back the students have left the school and we've completely taken over.

Two flights of stairs run either side of the audience seating and they take you into the school itself. We've commandeered a few classrooms. One is for the make-up artists. They worked on last year's debate so know what to expect. More recently they worked on Doctor Who. I can only imagine the contrast.

I have my own room although I won't be using it to dress in because it has a glass window in the door. My name's printed on a piece of paper taped to the door and somebody has drawn a star beneath it. I'm touched. There are also some crisps, sweets and water. Other classrooms have been turned into green rooms for each of the leaders and their teams although apparently they have sandwiches too. I should be outraged but I won't be eating any of them anyway.

The leaders come to check their positions and cameras. Carwyn Jones jokes that the low lectern is a cruel trick on him. It's too low for him to lean on in that barrister manner he likes to deploy in the Assembly. More seriously there's a very bright TV light in his eyes. After an eye operation a few years ago, sustained bright studio lights can make his eyes water. He'd just had the op when I recorded my Face to Face interview with him in 2011 and as the credits rolled it looked like he was crying. He still jokes that I made him cry during an interview.

Neil Hamilton is late for his chance to check all this because he's been in the Assembly chamber. Perhaps mistakenly, UKIP had tabled a debate on immigration for this afternoon meaning he couldn't leave the chamber. He jokes to the other leaders, 'Where were you?'

The audience has been arriving, about two hundred or so who've all been checked for political allegiances or none. They're signing in and gathering in the school canteen for coffee and biscuits. Clearly school canteens have changed a lot since my day. It's shiny, stylish and spacious, more like an upmarket coffee shop. There's a good buzz of anticipation.

I go back to my classroom/green room and take a few bites of a Double Decker I'd bought earlier. I can't eat much before a major event like this but I'll need some energy and as a result of years of experience I can confirm that Double Deckers are by far the best thing for an energy boost.

The audience are led in and have taken their seats, the cameras are all in place and there are final 'good lucks' being said by everyone on stage and in the talkback in my ear. It's time to begin.

The leaders are ranged either side of me. On my immediate left is Andrew RT Davies and next to him Neil Hamilton. On my right is Carwyn Jones, Leanne Wood and Mark Williams.

I ask a light-hearted question to warm us all up. Since we're in a school, I ask them what their memories are of school days and whether or not they were good students. I've forgotten that Mark Williams was a deputy head teacher before becoming an MP so his memories of school are more recent.

At 8 o'clock, I stand on the edge of the stage, just feet away from the first row of audience members. There's a tense quiet in my ear as the production team wait for the countdown to begin and there's a hush in the hall. It's strange to think that in seconds we'll be live on ITV and online as well as being involved in two hours of loud and sometimes robust debate. Then comes the count, 5, 4, 3, 2, 1 and I say,

'This General Election looks like being one of the most momentous ever. A huge amount will be at stake when you cast your vote in three weeks' time. Tonight, live on this stage, five Welsh leaders will try to persuade us to vote for their party. This is the ITV Wales Election Debate.'

After the titles I say, 'Good evening from Stanwell School in the Vale of Glamorgan. We're here live for the next two hours to learn more about what each of the main Welsh political parties are offering. They want our votes on June the 8th. Tonight we find out why they think they deserve them.'

We play a video montage of how we got here. There are shots of Jeremy Corbyn and Theresa May campaigning. There's a clip of Carwyn Jones saying, 'What have the Tories ever done for Wales?', Leanne Wood claiming that, 'There are a lot of people who are very, very angry', and Neil Hamilton saying, 'I'm up for the fight.' We see Boris Johnson, Paul Nuttall, Christina Rees, Mark Williams and Tim Farron. Andrew RT Davies is shown saying, 'We have to fight for every square foot of turf in Wales.'

The leaders have opening statements of a minute each. Then we play the video introduction to our first questioner, who is Callum McSorley. He's only just turned eighteen so will be a first time voter and is appropriately a student at Stanwell School. In his VT he says that he feels overwhelmed and worried that he doesn't have all the facts and figures to make a fully informed decision. His question is deceptively simple: 'As a first time voter trying to make sense of Brexit why should I vote for your party?'

In the debate, Mark Williams displays a fierceness that surprises those used only to his mild manners. He makes his apology for the Lib Dem tuition fee debacle and delivers forcefully a defence of immigration and a second referendum.

Leanne Wood scores points with the sort of carefully-timed jibes that she first demonstrated against Nigel Farage in 2015. When Williams says there'll be no coalition she says, to loud cheers, 'There is: the Tories and UKIP.' She's the most-experienced of all of those on stage tonight when it comes to taking part in TV debates.

Davies' use of the phrase 'strong and stable' starts to get loud groans from the audience. At one stage the groan is almost a cheer. His final use of it gets a small round of applause as well.

A man in a Union flag-patterned suit gets annoyed at the politicians talking over each other and voices his opinion loudly. 'We're not school kids here,' he shouts. 'We're adults. Can we behave like it please.' Wood replies, 'Well said,' but remains as assiduous at interrupting as any of the others.

I make a couple of school-related quips, threatening detention or letters home. In fact they're very unruly and shout over each other a lot. We've already decided we'll be more relaxed this time about letting them interrupt and challenge each other but there are points when I worry it could just become noise. 'There's only so much shouting we can do and I can do,' I say at one point to Davies but it could have been to any of them.

As the moderator, you have to be ready to interrupt people for time reasons as much as anything else. There will always be those who think that you're biased for or against one or another and you have to accept that. But you also have to be comfortable letting them have a pop at each other. By the third debate I was more relaxed about allowing them to argue with each other but you can't let it go on too long. In the theatre and particularly on the stage it can feel quite exciting when they talk over each other but you have to realise that if you're watching on TV or online after a while it just becomes noise.

The discussion on immigration is the most fiery. The question comes from Stephen Tull, a maths teacher whose wife is Polish and works in the NHS. He says that after the referendum, his wife suddenly felt unwelcome in the country she had considered home. He wants to know about the future for people like his wife and British citizens abroad.

During the ad break, the audience take over. The questioner, Stephen, takes issue with something Neil Hamilton had said, asking if his Eastern European wife is 'a problem.' As Hamilton starts to answer him, he and others start saying loudly 'disgusting.'

A young woman tells how her pregnant sister can't rejoin her family in the UK and begins crying. Different groups in the audience then start challenging each other.

They only just quieten down when the final part begins. In the discussion, about trust in politicians, Davies attacks Labour for spending 'the last eighteen months ripping itself apart' and asks if anyone could 'seriously believe that Jeremy Corbyn can run a government that will stand up for this country.'

This is too much for one member of the audience who shouts repeated demands for the extra £350m a week for the NHS promised by Leave campaigners. He gets a big cheer from the audience. Davies tries to answer but the man keeps shouting. Hamilton's answer, about the decision being up to the government of the day, elicits hissing. The man keeps shouting. I thank him for his contribution but move on because I can't allow it to take over the last ten minutes of the debate.

Moments like that and audience interaction certainly add excitement to the occasion although this year's audience was significantly more willing to shout out than the audiences for the previous two debates who confined themselves to boos and cheers.

Then it's all over. The atmosphere is still tingling. There are handshakes and hugs and everyone's relieved and pleased. People keep asking me if I enjoyed it or how I thought it went. I can't tell. While it's happening, it's just a question of getting through it all. A group of University of South Wales students come on stage for selfies with me.

I head up the stairs from the stage to the back of the theatre and into the body of the school where our classroom/green rooms are. Before I get to the top I see Carwyn Jones and his special adviser Huw Price at the top and coming toward me. They're ashen-faced and I hear the First Minister say to Huw, 'Here's Adrian, we can tell Adrian.'

My heart sinks. My first thought is that they have a very serious complaint but they don't look angry so maybe someone's said something very wrong, maybe a libel? My mind races back over the last two hours, but I just can't think of what could have gone so badly wrong. Then Carwyn says quietly, 'Rhodri's dead.'

I'm stunned. 'What?'

'We don't know how he died, whether or not it was a heart attack or he was knocked off his bike. But it's happened this evening.' [21]

In the school canteen there are conflicting atmospheres. Red faces and tears in the eyes of Labour people, shock and upset in the faces of others who've been told, and frantic activity by producers. Owain is about to go live into the news and has now

---

[21] That weekend, Carwyn Jones described in the Sunday Times how he heard the news of Rhodri Morgan's death, his first thought similar to mine:

'On Thursday evening, I'd just finished a live TV debate for the general election when my media adviser appeared next to me with an ashen face. I assumed I'd made some terrible faux pas. Like the rest of Wales, I was unprepared for the news he imparted: Rhodri Morgan had died suddenly.'

That media adviser, Huw Price, later confirmed that account. He told me that Carwyn Jones had seen his face and said to him, 'What did I do wrong?'

had to change everything he planned to say. He's also borrowed a black tie from James. Meanwhile the chatter and argument about the debate continues.

The UKIP man in a union flag suit who'd been one of the most vociferous hecklers stops to continue making his points. Amongst the Conservatives, Vince raises concern about the last section of debate, saying that it was confusing because it was about devolved matters. He also complains that journalists in the spin room didn't want to speak to the senior figures he'd brought. Shattered and drained, I say, 'I'm responsible for many things but not that,' and he laughs.

Afterwards we gather in a bar for a few pints to go over the night, the debate and to remember Rhodri Morgan.

Rob Osborne recalls when he was a student journalist and managed to wangle his way into Welsh Government press conferences. Even though he was First Minister, unlike most other AMs, Rhodri always took an interest in what Rob and the other students were doing and made time for them to interview him, even though he knew nobody would ever hear it.

That matched my own early memories of him. He regularly made time for a know-nothing commercial radio journalist and not just to give comments, but to gossip too and in turn to pump me for information.

I remember too, years later, when I was presenting the Politics Show one Sunday on BBC Wales. He was due to be the main interviewee and we'd been told he could only record it a few hours before the programme went on air. The time came and went and phone calls went unanswered. Eventually he was tracked down to the garden and we were told he'd come in live. He did, wearing his gardening gear which included a muddy Cuba sweatshirt and yes, he went on air dressed that way. Nobody questioned why the First Minister of Wales would be on a Sunday politics programme dressed for the garden. That's because nobody would have been in the least surprised.

At conferences it's customary for journalists to be given hard copies of the main speeches just before they're delivered. Once at a Welsh Labour conference I asked Jo Kiernan, his special adviser for just such a copy. She said she had no idea what he was going to say. It may have been that conference when he started praising NHS standards by remembering how much worse they'd been when he was young, recalling using a milk bottle to urinate in. I was sitting on the floor and looked across the hall to Jo who was also sitting on the floor. She simply shrugged.

It was only last month that I recorded an episode of Welsh Bites with Rhodri. I knew even then that it was an extraordinary interview – he spoke about things in a way I hadn't heard from him before.[22]

We keep talking past midnight. We're all shattered and dazed. The debate, which finished just hours ago and everybody thinks went well, is a distant memory.

---

[22] A re-edited version was eventually shown with the consent of his family as Rhodri Morgan: the Last Interview.

The Last Interview

Just over a month before he died, I'd filmed an episode of 'Adrian's Welsh Bites' with Rhodri Morgan. In these programmes I interview a guest while cooking with them. Well, 'cooking' is stretching it with some of the guests and certainly when it comes to my appalling culinary skills. Rhodri was no slouch in the kitchen though. After he retired from politics, he took on the role of main cook and famously made sandwiches for Julie who continued as an Assembly Member.

I knew the interview was out of the ordinary, even before it became a poignant one. He spoke about his own experiences and some of his thinking in a way that I hadn't heard him do before. I guess the experience of writing his memoirs had crystallised his memories and thoughts.

It was quite something for me too. I'd been interviewing him on and off for my whole career as a journalist. We'd been in informal situations for off-the-record chats, a coffee or a glass of wine at his Christmas receptions or at Welsh Night at Labour conferences. I'd never been in his home though or really spent so much time with him. With hindsight he seemed tired on occasions and was certainly glad that we left in time for him to have a nap before picking his grandson up, but even when he was in government he'd made no secret of his belief in power-naps.

There was a lot of talk about gardening. Before we started cooking, he took me into the garden to pick herbs and rhubarb for our dessert.

While we were preparing the food, I couldn't resist stealing bits of the cheese I was grating which led to one of my favourite moments when he said, 'I always planned it to go on my own terms in my own time, leaving my successor plenty of time to put his – Stop it, Adrian. Now. Leave it alone.'

He described how unique political circumstances aligned to make the Assembly a reality. 'Devolution had been such a struggle to get going [that] I just felt that I was very, very fortunate to be in the right place at the right time when devolution finally did happen. You know we had a window really, and I mean, it may be that that the window in 1997 ... was [the] window. You couldn't have done it afterwards and you couldn't have done it before and I happened to be the lucky person who was in the right place at the right time.'

He talked about falling out with the entire New Labour hierarchy:

'Well obviously something happened in those, probably the last two years of Opposition from '95 to '97. I managed to have a quarrel with Peter Mandelson, I managed to have a quarrel with David Miliband, I managed to have a quarrel with Alastair Campbell. I managed to have a quarrel with pretty well everybody that had the Prime Minister's ear. How I managed that I do not know.'

We talked about his heart attack in July 2007. I said that I'd been reporting on the coalition talks between Labour and Plaid Cymru and then all of a sudden, he wasn't there.

'Politics stopped for a day. They told me, you have to have complete rest for three weeks. I said I can't have a rest for three weeks because I'm bloody forming a government.' Then he joked how 'It was the easiest cabinet ever to form – every candidate was told, do not argue with the First Minister he might keel over... Everyone was meek as can be.'

When I once asked him on a TV programme if there was such a thing as Morganism, he just laughed. But he came close to explaining it in this interview – spelling out Clear Red Water as a political philosophy.

'When I look up at what's happening in Scotland now I often feel that one of the problems has been that people define themselves as either nationalist or unionist. I would never describe myself as a unionist because the unionists were the people who were against devolution in the first place whereas if you're a nationalist obviously you don't believe in devolution because you think it doesn't goes far enough and you want to become a completely different country. But it's this, trying to define this space of being passionate about devolution. Not seeing it as a halfway house to independence or anything that's been conceded to the nationalists because otherwise there'd be problems. It's actually a belief that the British constitution is much healthier for having devolution since 1999.'

'So it's an end in itself rather than a means to an end?'

'It's an end itself, yes exactly.'

THURSDAY 18TH MAY

There's no time to recover from last night's debate. Today will be one of the most momentous of my career of covering Welsh politics.

A book of condolences for Rhodri Morgan has been opened in the Senedd and flags are flying at half mast. There'll be a minute's silence at 12.30 for AMs and staff.

I go through the Welsh Bites programme which was postponed when the election was called and has been partially edited. It's strange to see the two of us in the garden picking herbs and rhubarb, chatting in the kitchen and eating the food that we've just prepared. I choose a couple of clips for tonight's news.

We learn from police that he died while cycling in country lanes near his home. He was pronounced dead at the scene.

All parties agree on a pause in campaigning for the election out of respect.

I go to Paul Flynn's house to interview him about Rhodri Morgan. He has some glorious anecdotes from years of working with him and sharing an office with him. When they both were first elected, a photo call was arranged of them leaving for London from Cardiff Central station along with Alun Michael. The other newly-elected Labour MP Paul Murphy was to meet them at Newport. Rhodri Morgan arrived with his change of clothes in some Tesco bags (a lot of stories about him seem to involve Tesco bags) which Flynn felt didn't look the part up against the new suitcases of the other two. So he (Flynn) took them and hid them out of camera shot. The three new MPs got on the train and left for London without Rhodri Morgan's Tesco Bags, shirts and other clothes which remained hidden on Cardiff railway station until he could retrieve them several days later.

Inevitably though we talk about the election and his own prospects, as we sit in a dining room filled with boxes of leaflets.

'By any sensible consideration, I'm toast,' he says, adding that he's told his staff to be prepared to be out of work. He says he's written to Jeremy Corbyn as 'an old friend and colleague' to warn that 'it ain't going to happen and it's because of you. That's what they're telling us on the doorstep – it's him, that they just don't like him, the not wearing a tie, etc. These things matter to our voters more than any others.'

Having said that, Flynn hasn't given up. Some Conservatives upset by the Newport West selection row have said they'll vote for him. He says the local Tory party was threatened with winding-up if it didn't select Angela Jones-Evans. Plaid people have said they'll vote for him, Greens too. His dry humour never fails him. 'It would be very unfair of the voters to bring my young parliamentary career to a halt at the tender age of eighty-two.'

Tonight's Wales at Six is given over to Rhodri Morgan. Andrea presents from the Senedd where I join her. I begin my report with pictures of politicians and staff standing in silence in the spot where we're broadcasting.

We have archive footage of him becoming First Secretary (as the title then was) in February 2000, amongst his first comments a joke about the unsettled political atmosphere that had brought him to the job: 'My number one target as First Secretary is to survive until the half term recess at the end of this week.'

As I say on air, it's easy to forget just how unloved and uncertain the Assembly was in those early days and how much he did to settle it and establish it. I include a clip of Carwyn Jones saying that, 'He took a fledgling, young democracy – it was very fragile, things had not gone well in 2000 – and built an institution and a government on top of that.'

We run the clips from the unbroadcast Welsh Bites programme, including that in which he tells me to stop pinching the cheese that I'm grating. After it I say, 'I've been told off by First Ministers in lots of different circumstances, but never for nicking the cheese.'

It's the ITV Leaders' Debate in Salford. I was due to be there to cover it in person before events intervened. It's a strange affair without Theresa May and Jeremy Corbyn. Paul Nuttall keeps calling Leanne Wood 'Natalie' which leads to the response: 'I'm not Natalie, I'm Leanne.' I notice she uses the Gibraltar line she used in our debate.

Before tonight, one of the production team asked me where the areas of disagreement are likely to be between Leanne Wood and Nicola Sturgeon. Not many was my answer, but tonight they disagree over class sizes. Sturgeon says she wants class sizes to be as small as possible while Wood says there's no evidence that class sizes make any difference to outcome.

"The Welsh alpha-male par excellence."

In the Bites programme I made with him, Rhodri Morgan told me that he'd never been tempted by the prospect of a peerage and in fact had turned down two offers.

'I always said if I'd wanted to stay in politics then I would have stayed in the same job that I had before of being First Minister but if I want to hand over to the younger generation I don't want to be then having the so called platform of being able to speak on issues in the House of Lords. I'd feel a fraud.'

However, I did see him in the House of Lords once. During the

time of the Conservative-Liberal Democrat government, the Lords'
Constitution Committee was looking into other examples of parties
working together. Rhodri Morgan and Ieuan Wyn Jones were invited
to give evidence. They'd always worked well together as First Minister
and Deputy First Minister.

When I arrived at the committee room, which was at the farthest
end of Parliament's committee corridor, I found them sitting next to
each other on a bench, reading through their notes, comfortable with
each other, political opponents who'd ended up allies.

In front of the committee, Ieuan Wyn Jones revealed how the trust
had been built up a long time before they formed a coalition government in 2007.

'My first experience of working with civil servants in Wales was in
2003 when Rhodri, as First Minister, wrote to me and said, 'We

would like you to consider whether you want to have a discussion with civil servants about manifesto commitments.' I took that offer up, and I built up a good relationship with him, in the sense that the then permanent secretary designated the civil servant to work with us. I was confident that none of the stuff I discussed with him would be discussed anywhere else. By the time we came to 2007, I was confident that, if I called on the civil servant to give me advice, then I would accept it.'

Rhodri Morgan's comments in that committee attracted some attention because he said that coalition could still have happened between Labour and the Liberal Democrats in 2010 but he would have advised Gordon Brown that he had to step down to make it possible.

His former sparring partner, Lord Crickhowell described him as 'The Welsh alpha-male par excellence.' He didn't seem to take offence.

SUNDAY 21ST MAY

It looks like my moaning has paid off when a text arrives saying, 'You are sorted with PM interview.' I'm not sure when or where this is likely to happen.

Nick texts: 'Op note just dropped: north Wales.' Another text from a Conservative assures me it'll be Wrexham, another seat the Conservatives are sure they can win.[23] A later email from CCHQ says, 'There will be the opportunity for Adrian to get a clip (couple of questions) with the PM after the speech.' I'll see how far I can push 'a couple of questions.'

---

[23] Actually, Gresford

According to the preview extracts, she's going to use her visit to warn how close the Brexit negotiations are and to present what she says is a stark choice:

Every vote for me and my team in this election will be a vote to strengthen my hand in the negotiations to come. Every vote for any other party – Labour, the Liberal Democrats or Plaid Cymru – is a vote to send Jeremy Corbyn into the negotiating chamber on our behalf.

She'll bring together a familiar Conservative criticism of Labour taking the people of Wales for granted with an unusual new attack on all Remain supporting politicians (apart from herself). The preview continues:

And I know that sense of disenchantment is particularly acute here in Wales. We saw that when people here in Wrexham and across Wales chose to ignore the hysterical warnings of Labour, Plaid Cymru and Liberal Democrat politicians in Cardiff Bay, and voted to leave the EU.

It's a clear attempt to refocus people's minds after a dreadful few days for the Tories whose policy of making elderly people in England pay for their own care from the combined value of their savings and houses (apart from £100,000 and not while they're still alive) has been the main talking point. It's been called the 'Death Tax', a term that the Tories used against Labour so successfully in 2015 and, perhaps more damningly, 'Dementia Tax', because it's more likely to affect people who need more expensive dementia care. Social care is devolved and there's a different system here in Wales, but that doesn't seem to be making any difference to the discussion.

Reading the news today has made it clear that many Tories think it's morally wrong and bad politics too because it puts off many of their natural supporters. There are other commentators though who say it's brave and even 'progressive' because it acknowledges the cost of social care and the fact that many pensioners are, if not well-off, living in houses with a lot of equity.

It's clearly had an effect on the polls. UK surveys published today show the Conservative lead halved.

Perfect timing for another one of ours then and when the news comes through it doesn't disappoint. Well, it'll disappoint the Conservatives.

Nick texts to say, 'Poll puts Lab on 44% Con 34%.'

My reply: 'Woah!'

This is a complete switch from our first poll which showed the Conservatives in the lead. The second showed Labour closing the gap and now this. Given when the polling was carried out I think it must reflect the impact of the social care row even though that's about an England-only policy. It might also have something to do with the death of Rhodri Morgan and the fact that much of the coverage has reminded people of the way that he tried to establish Welsh Labour as something different to the party at a UK level.

MONDAY 22ND MAY

I catch an early train to Wrexham.

There should be an added frisson to this event because it's become clear over the weekend just how badly the Conservative manifesto proposals for pensioners (the 'triple whammy') particularly the social care policy are going down with Conservatives as much as anyone else. There's already speculation that she'll make a U-turn. Will she do it here?

I'm nearly not allowed into the Village Hall in Gresford because I've left my ID in my bag in the satellite truck. Richard Minshull, the chair of the Welsh Conservatives, has to step in and vouch for me. There are a hundred or so activists and almost as many journalists and camera crews it seems. As well as there being a lot of police officers in the car park, outside the hall and waiting inside.

Theresa May's large election bus is having some difficulty turning around in the small car park. A dreadlocked protester is dragged off by police shouting, 'This is the fascist state that we're living in.'

News of our poll has filtered through to those there. One senior figure tells me he's being realistic about their prospects but still thinks gains will be made. As for the other parties, 'I'm keeping my eye on Plaid in Blaenau Gwent.'

The candidate in Alyn and Deeside, Laura Knightly tells me, 'It does feel different [to 2015].' I ask how she rates her chances: 'Good, but I'm taking nothing for granted. It does feel different. People are saying they voted Labour then but they'll vote for us this time.'

A senior Conservative says to me with some glee, 'Your poll's a shocker isn't it? It'll be a kick up the arse for some of them. It'll wipe the smile off their faces.'

Another tells me they can't believe the poll and think it must be a mistake although not unhelpful, a wake-up call for those who've become complacent.

The manifesto is already causing problems but the Tory I talk to says that rather than the social care policy, it's the winter fuel payments policy that people are really upset about.

But they add, 'I still think it'll be Corbyn that'll cost Labour.' A man came up to me in Ruthin – the Secretary of the local Labour branch. He said, 'I can't vote for Jeremy Corbyn. I can't vote for you lot and you're going to win anyway so I'm voting Plaid. I think we'll still win a few seats up here.'

One of Theresa May's advisors says hello and 'Sorry about

Bridgend, it wasn't good enough. Glad to have sorted you out with an interview. There'll be a media Q & A too – feel free to put your hand up.' He won't be drawn on our poll saying only that, 'It's hard to read into individual polls.' I think he has bigger worries on his mind, namely what seem to be increasing problems with the manifesto.

I take my seat amongst the extremely large number of journalists. Unexpectedly, the former Labour MP Sian James is sitting behind me. She's working with some of my colleagues to produce a programme for S4C. I ask her how it feels. She says, 'It's weird. I keep thinking about thirty years ago [when she was active in the miners' strike.] I probably wouldn't have been allowed here.'

The audience is similar to that in Bridgend: Conservatives from across the north, candidates and campaigners. Former Welsh Secretary David Jones is here. But there's no sign of Andrew RT Davies. I ask but something is muttered about him being on holiday. It seems odd at the launch of a Welsh manifesto.

It's a funny Welsh manifesto though. I skim through it and can't see much that is particularly Welsh in it. Certainly nothing stands out.

While the Stereophonics song 'Have a Nice Day' is playing, the buzz amongst the journalists is that a U-turn is about to come.

Theresa May comes on stage and delivers some familiar lines about asking voters for 'the strong hand you grant me by supporting my candidates in this election.' She tells them there's no time to waste.

She says the Welsh manifesto 'is a plan to make Wales and our Union stronger.' She uses the phrase I heard from a party source a couple of weeks ago: 'Too often in the past, UK Governments have tended to 'devolve and forget'. The government I lead will put that right.' Some will welcome that approach; others will see it as interference. Either way she lists the sort of actions the UK government's taking or will take to help Wales.

She makes the previewed but still strange attack on the 'hysterical warnings' of all Remain campaigners other than herself and makes her own warning that, 'A loss of just six seats will cost my Government our majority and create a hung Parliament... Nothing but chaos.'

Then comes the U-turn, although you wouldn't know it was one from what she says. No it's merely a clarification, she says, and she's only making it because of 'Jeremy Corbyn's fake claims.'

An activist turns to me and says, 'There are more press than punters here.' And there is a lot. They only have one thing to ask though and it's extraordinary to see it happen. One after another asks variations on the same question, how damaging are her manifesto policies for older people and how unusual is it to make a U-turn during an election campaign. She gets increasingly frustrated and finally flings her arms out to repeat, 'Nothing has changed.'

I get my five minutes with her. Once again she denies there's been a U-turn: 'No there has been no change to the principles on social care policy that we set out in our manifesto. I'm very clear: we have an aging society, there'll be two million more people aged over seventy-five in just a decade. Our social care system will collapse if we don't address this problem.'

I interrupt to say that a cap wasn't in the manifesto. She ignores the interruption. 'That's what I'm doing, I'm addressing the challenge we face of an aging society.'

I raise what she said in her speech about 'the hysterical warnings' of Leave campaigners in the other parties. I point out to her, though she surely hasn't forgotten, that she campaigned to remain too so how can people trust her?

'I did campaign for Remain, but across the whole United Kingdom, people voted to leave the European Union. I and my party are the only party that are absolutely committed to respect the will of the people of Wales and the people of the United Kingdom.'

That brings me onto the question of EU funding; what will happen to the aid given to Wales when control of that money reverts to Westminster? Hints dropped by senior Conservatives such as Alun Cairns suggest that the proposed replacement, the Shared Prosperity fund will not necessarily give Wales the priority it's enjoyed in terms of aid. It looks like Wales will have to compete with English regions for money it currently gets to itself.

Theresa May says to me, 'What this is about is making sure tax-payer money is spent effectively and in the interests of ordinary working people.'

But would Wales have to compete for those funds?

'It will be about ensuring that the disparities that exist between our four nations and within those nations are being addressed. That means that decisions being taken in relation to funding for Wales and other parts of the United Kingdom will be funding decisions that will be in the interests of ordinary working people.'

But Wales would have to compete with English regions?

'The Shared Prosperity fund will work with all the devolved administrations.'

I take that as a yes.

Afterwards the candidate Andrew Atkinson is waiting to have his photo with the PM but because of the protestors outside the building, she's smuggled out the back. He looks disappointed. But he says he's quietly confident about taking Wrexham. He says, 'It's looking good,' and that there's evidence of people switching straight from Labour to Conservatives.

While Theresa May is sort of launching the Welsh Conservative manifesto in Gresford, Welsh Labour is nearby in Mold launching its manifesto. If it was confusing that most of the Tory event was focussed on a policy that doesn't apply in Wales, Labour's pledges are confusing in the other direction: three of its five main pledges relate to devolved areas that voting in this election won't affect in the slightest.

And while the Conservatives' UK leader is at their launch but the Welsh leader isn't, the opposite is true of Labour. Its Welsh leader is there but not its UK leader. Owain is there for us and tackles Carwyn Jones about Jeremy Corbyn's absence both from the event and from the pages of the manifesto. The First Minister says, 'He is inside it but it's a Welsh Labour manifesto so people expect the leader of Welsh Labour to be on the front. But we are a party that works in partnership in Westminster and Cardiff Bay.'

Then I get the train back. While I'm on the train, our poll is published. Just before it goes online, I tweet that people should be sitting down. As it's published I tweet: 'Take another deep breath.'

As well as the switch around in Conservative and Labour support, the poll also suggests it's ceasing to be a single issue election as other issues than Brexit are becoming more important.

In his now regular interview for us, Roger says, 'Jeremy Corbyn is still not doing fantastically well as Labour leader, polling relatively poorly in Wales for a Labour leader. We do see however that Carwyn Jones is performing particularly strongly and this validates the Labour party in Wales and their decision to make Carwyn Jones front and centre of the Welsh Labour campaign.'

Nick and I work on the script together via email and phone conversations. However, the train, which was already going to be tight, is delayed. Then the taxi I take from the station is held up by heavy traffic because of Champions League security so I abandon the cab and half walk/half run. I get into the office at 5.30, record my voiceover and go into the studio. On air I talk about shock and disbelief amongst Conservatives, Labour and the other parties at such an incredible turnaround. I highlight the row over social care, the focus on Labour being different after the death of Rhodri Morgan. Conservatives are still seen as strongest on Brexit, I say, but other issues, notably health, are suddenly becoming important and that could be good news for Labour. I remark that it's looking increasingly like a two-party election.

I learn that Rhodri Morgan's funeral is likely to be held next Wednesday. It's a surprise that the Senedd is the location. No funeral has ever been held there before but it's perfectly appropriate.

For Sharp End, Chris Davies is a last minute replacement. I'd heard that morning in Gresford that the party was having difficulty finding someone to step in to be the Conservative on our panel. Some of them have apparently simply refused to do it. Chris jokes, 'They're all keeping their heads down and they've left it to me to deal with social care.'

He certainly gets a lot of grief about the 'Dementia Tax' during the programme from the other guests. He says they're ramping it up as a problem and defends the policy.

The Conservative Manifesto

Nobody doubts it but some of them still can't quite believe it. When I ask politicians of all parties when they noticed things change they say one word. 'Manifesto.' And they mean the Conservative manifesto.

One unsuccessful candidate that I bumped into in Westminster after the election told me, 'It was a combination of ours and theirs [Labour's]. It took a weekend, but the change was clear.'

A senior MP backed that up. 'We had a manifesto that didn't work. One of the things I noticed in particular was that the mood of the election changed abruptly on the day after the manifesto was published. It was as dramatic as that. The day after the manifesto was published we were knocking on doors in good areas for us and we were immediately getting challenged on the manifesto, people were saying, 'we don't like your manifesto.'

In particular the party's policy on paying for social care in England went down extremely badly. One senior Welsh Tory told me the policy was good and defensible but not within a snap election campaign. Another pointed out that they'd also read 'some brilliant defences of the poll tax' which was another political disaster.

Another senior Conservative agreed that it was a pivotal moment but blames successful Labour portrayal rather than the policy itself. Describing it to me, they clicked their fingers and said, 'It was like flicking a switch.

'We knew that people were being whipped up by Labour or other parties who were saying 'they're going to have your house you know. It doesn't surprise me that they were doing that but there was this huge gap between what they were saying and a policy that was determined to address these structural challenges we have over older age care.

'Some people were knocking doors and they were saying, 'I'm not going to vote for you, you're going to take my house from me on June the 9th.' So starting in that position, trying to explain a policy, explain why they should elect Byron Davies or whoever is a big ask.'

Then there was the U-turn in Gresford: 'It was a really bad policy and it was made worse by the Prime Minister's explanation of the policy at Gresford,' said one MP. 'She actually handled it rather badly because it was quite clear she was going to have to row back on the policy because it had been so shredded over the weekend that she had to do something about it. But I think it was the turn of phrase, 'Nothing has changed' that actually went down particularly badly because it was perfectly clear that there had been a change of heart.'

One Welsh Tory describes the Gresford launch as a 'shit show' and it's true that Labour campaign co-ordinators couldn't believe their *luck: 'You have a UK Prime Minister coming to Wales to an event where her Welsh Tory leader wasn't invited, to backtrack on a policy that didn't apply in Wales to begin with.'*

The way Labour found out what was happening to their opponents at the event sounds like a scene from 'The Thick of It.' Senior members of the campaign team weren't far from Gresford because Labour's Welsh manifesto launch was taking place near Mold. A team member described it to me:

'There was no wifi, we were huddled in a classroom in an agricultural college, running the Mirror website. I tethered my iphone to a laptop to get it but I could only get a signal by standing on a table. So I was stood on a table holding my phone up, the others were watching it on the laptop and we were just going, 'Is this actually happening? Fucking hell, Andrew RT's not there. Fucking hell she's saying nothing's changed and while all of this is happening, the MPs arrive so I'm standing there on a table holding my phone in the air and then senior Welsh MPs and Welsh Government ministers walk in and we kept thinking, they can't be doing it, no.. they're doing it... they're doing it. And then Alun Cairns ran away from Laura Kuenssberg.'

TUESDAY 23RD MAY

I wake to news of an appalling attack on Manchester. Twenty-two people are dead. The UK parties have suspended their election campaigning and nobody's sure for how long. There's even talk of postponing the election itself. I check with the Welsh parties who are all doing the same.

Today in the Assembly was already due to be an unusual one because tributes to Rhodri Morgan were planned. I email the Assembly Commission press office and am told that they're looking at making changes and allowing a vigil to take place on the Senedd steps. The changes involve statements on the Manchester attack from the Presiding Officer and First Minister and a minute's silence. Then AMs will pay tribute to Rhodri Morgan. Julie Morgan may be in the chamber. After that there'll be another silence, a break after which normal Assembly business, including FMQs, will take place. It'll all be finished by 5pm so that AMs can join the vigil.

When she speaks, the Llywydd Elin Jones, condemns an 'unforgivable act of violence.' Carwyn Jones says that he's been given a national security briefing by the Cabinet Office and that he's written to the Prime Minister and the Mayor of Manchester, 'expressing our outrage at the attacks and offering our solidarity with the people of Manchester.' Assembly members stand and the chamber falls silent.

Next, Elin Jones begins the tributes to Rhodri Morgan, saying, 'Many of us have lost a friend, and Wales has lost a political giant.' Carwyn Jones talks about how he learned of the news immediately after our debate last Wednesday. He says that he saw him as a father figure and that, 'what I am now as a politician, I owe to him.'

The Conservative leader tells how he first met Rhodri Morgan not in politics but as neighbours in rural Vale of Glamorgan. The First Minister, he says, was barricading his garden to stop Andrew RT Davies' cattle invading, but far from being irate, he was more interested in finding out what kind of cattle they were.

Leanne Wood says that, 'He ensured that the foundations of devolution were cemented to ensure that it would outlast his time as First Minister.'

Neil Hamilton describes the man he knew when they were both MPs and who was 'a fully paid-up member of the awkward squad.' He agrees with others' assessment of his legacy in devolution, saying that 'He did as much as anyone to establish this Assembly as a permanent feature of Welsh life, confounding the initial scepticism of people like me.'

Kirsty Williams' voice is wavering as she recounts that, 'When my mother passed away, he wrote not only to me but he wrote to my late father. My father couldn't believe that the First Minister of Wales had taken the time to write to him about his loss. He was a decent, decent man.'

After watching the TV feed from our Assembly office for a while, I move to the public gallery in the Senedd. Rhodri Morgan's brother, children, grandchildren and other family members are there along with MPs, former advisers, press officers and opponents.

Julie Morgan has been in her place in the chamber throughout the tributes. She's the last one called to speak and says, 'Losing Rhodri is a terrible personal blow to me and to the family. It is an aching loss, and I know that I haven't realised yet the full enormity.'

She's applauded by all the other AMs, the sound reverberating up into the public gallery where it's matched by applause from those gathered there. Everybody stands for another moment of silence after which the session is suspended for ten minutes.

I go back to our office, bumping into the Conservative AM Russell George who says that it'll be weird carrying on Assembly business as normal this afternoon. 'I already have questions tabled and I've rephrased them,' he says, adding that perhaps, 'there might be more meaningful debate.'

It's not quite business as usual. In First Minister's Questions, Leanne Wood concentrates on the implications of the Manchester attacks. Andrew RT Davies waives his right to ask three questions and also chooses to focus on security matters in his single question. Neil Hamilton does the same.

Nathan Gill comes out of the chamber and says, 'There's such a sombre mood in there, I hardly wanted to ask a question. Maybe Neil [Hamilton] is building bridges. He said, 'Good question' to me.'

Outside the Senedd, a couple of hundred people gather for the vigil organised by Churches Together. The First Minister and other politicians along with leaders from different faiths take part while I'm preparing to go live into the news.

I describe a day like no other, of tributes, of cross-party solidarity, of business not as usual, cut short to enable AMs to attend the vigil behind me. 'In a lot of ways,' I say, 'we've seen the very best of our politicians here today.'

Conservatives Fall Out

'Something about a holiday' doesn't even come close to explaining why Andrew RT Davies wasn't at the Conservative Welsh manifesto launch in Gresford but it's the answer I scribbled in my notebook when I asked about his absence.

There was a holiday involved as I write about elsewhere but there was much more to it than that. He had originally planned to be at the launch because he had also expected to take part in one of the BBC Wales election programmes nearby in Rhos-on-Sea.

However that weekend, the agreement between him and Alun Cairns had broken down when it was decided that Cairns should take part in 'Ask the Leader' instead of Davies. Two days before that programme, on the night of Saturday 20th May, a close aide to the Welsh Secretary rang Davies and told him the decision.

The Welsh Tory leader said, 'Look this has been handled appallingly. If you're going to bump me on Monday you've got to do the last debate, the main BBC one, and there's no way I'm going to come back [from holiday] and do that.'

The Cairns camp denied that Davies was bumped: 'What we signed up to was that if it was other AMs, it would be Andrew but the programme in Rhos was straight to the audience, it wasn't other AMs. I think actually BBC Wales were a bit cheeky and just piled it all in as one and said it would be easier.'

Some speculated that the Cairns team hadn't initially realised that 'Ask the Leader' wasn't a panel debate and only decided on the change when they did. Whatever the reason, it soon created a bigger problem. Davies was digging his heels in and refusing to back down over the BBC Wales debate. Those close to him believe that the party hierarchy hadn't appreciated 'the changes he'd made and the sacrifice he'd made to come back.'

The Tories had put themselves in an awkward position. Either Alun Cairns had to take part in the BBC debate or someone else had to be found.

Party officials were 'desperate not to be empty chaired' and agreed on two potential stand-ins with experience of TV debates, the MP for Monmouthshire, David TC Davies and the AM for Aberconwy, Darren Millar. Darren Millar was the person settled on although the decision undermined the 'skin in the game' argument. The counter argument was that he was the party's Director of Policy.

The statement issued the day that the row became a story was extraordinary saying that the Secretary of State was 'unwilling to take part.' There'd be even more extraordinary and angrier statements before long.

WEDNESDAY 24TH MAY

How things have changed: Assembly security staff are standing outside the building in the sun, checking passes before we even get inside to barriers and doors that require the same passes to open. They're friendly as always though. One tells me that their presence is more about reassuring people than clamping down.

I receive a lovely postcard from Labour stalwart and former adviser Ceri Williams. It has the brilliant Chalkie Davies photo of Ian Dury on the front. 'Dear Adrian, thanks to you and the team for the lovely tribute to Rhodri which made up yesterday's Wales at Six. It hit exactly the right note. Very classy.'

An anonymous letter arrives claiming 'dismay' among activists in Llanelli.

As you must now be aware, Plaid's candidate for the Llanelli Constituency is Cardiff-based businesswoman Mari Arthur, despite the choice of the local party at the hustings being local activist, Sean Rees. This, in itself, is a cause for dismay and the following points may illuminate the background to the imposition of Ms Arthur.

It goes on to make a series of allegations about the handling of the selection process which the author says illustrates, 'the democratic deficit of the process imposed on the Constituency.'

Another meeting about election night. We've decided to cover counts at Cardiff Central, West and North (where I'll be based for the network overnight programme), Ynys Môn, Ceredigion, Vale of Glamorgan, Swansea West, East and Gower, Delyn and Alyn and Deeside, Bridgend and Ogmore, Wrexham and Clwyd South, Newport West and East, Neath and Aberavon, Rhondda.

We're thinking of Vale of Clwyd, Cardiff South and Penarth, Blaenau Gwent, Llanelli and Carmarthen East.

I chat to a couple of Labour AMs. One of the areas we discuss is my home town. One of them says, 'Newport East is looking tight but better than it was. I don't think they'll take it. Newport West is different because it has a substantial Tory vote. I don't know how the terror threat will play out but they will hammer Jeremy Corbyn for "leadership."'

Another says that Clwyd South is not looking as bad as polls suggest. They reckon tactical voting will help and tell me that, 'Dafydd El has written a letter to be sent to key areas urging them to vote Susan to keep out the Tories and the Greens have decided not to put anyone up.'[24]

Another senior Labour person tells Nick that resistance to Corbyn is lessening.

"They saw the bits they needed to see."

It seems difficult to believe. Welsh Conservatives in Cardiff Bay didn't get to see the final draft of the party's Welsh manifesto before it was published at that fateful launch in Gresford. Their involvement was strictly limited. 'We fed into devolved aspects,' I was told.

As it happens there was very little difference between the UK manifesto which had already been published and the Welsh version so Welsh Tories would have known as much of it as anyone else who'd followed news coverage of the UK launch. And I'd been told during the election that Alun Cairns was closely involved in the manifesto process on matters related to Wales, such as pushing for the Severn

---

[24] Lord Dafydd Elis-Thomas, former Plaid Cymru leader, former Presiding Officer who left his party earlier in the year. It had previously been reported that he'd written a similar letter for distribution in Cardiff West.; Susan Elan Jones, the defending MP for Clwyd South.

Bridge tolls policy to be included. Even so, most observers would have expected at least some final say for the party's directly-elected Assembly leader and his team on a document they'd be defending in Wales. But no, they didn't see the final draft. Or the final copy.

A UK government source told me that, 'Very, very few people saw that manifesto. The Welsh Conservatives saw all the relevant devolved areas that were set to apply in Wales. They saw everything they needed to see. Very few people saw more than that. I think most people saw the bit they needed to see. Ministers in the UK Government only saw the bits they needed to see and then the manifesto was presented. And that was the decision taken by the central party to keep it close.'

I brought this up with a senior Tory MP who didn't think it an issue that Andrew RT Davies and his team didn't see the final document. 'I'm not entirely sure why they should. I didn't get sight of it either. The Welsh manifesto was not significantly different. I don't think that frankly it would have changed in Wales if people had been sighted of the manifesto or anything else. I don't think it would have made a shred of difference.'

THURSDAY 25TH MAY

I meet a senior Labour figure who's close to the campaign in Wales at an upscale cafe in a Cardiff suburb. We take a seat in a corner that's lined with shelves crammed with books, photos and imported pasta, flour and bottled sauces. Over the course of the next couple of hours we talk about how the campaign is going for Labour, how much distancing or otherwise is going on and what are the likely outcomes. Despite having fought many campaigns, this person describes 'an election like no other I've ever experienced' and one that's changed hugely already and looks likely to change again.

At this stage, I ask, what sort of campaign is it?

'Objectively, it's still a question of how big the Tory majority will be. We're still fighting a defensive campaign. The Tories don't expect such a massive majority or they wouldn't still be working Bridgend, Newport West and Cardiff West. Bridgend isn't gone. We haven't given up anywhere. It'll be nothing of the order of a landslide for the Tories.'

I ask about the strategy of distancing the party in Wales from the party at a UK level. My coffee companion tells me there's something even more interesting at play, something that hasn't happened in British politics before.

'The Welsh Labour thing' – we've had some hard press from some journalists but it reflects a reality that's come true, this time more than at any other time. The Labour party in Wales has changed and the party has learned lessons from Scotland. There'll be no going back after the election.

'We've been trying to develop a working relationship between Carwyn Jones and Sadiq Khan, by-passing the Labour central machine. Labour is changing. Andy Burnham, Sadiq Khan and Carwyn Jones are alternative poles of leadership. London-based. Westminster commentators tend to marginalise these but it's the reality. People in those areas look as much to those leaders as to the UK leadership.

'More work has gone into the Welsh manifesto than any other

Welsh manifesto and there's been no interference. Everything Carwyn Jones asked for in the Clause V meeting, he got.

'It's a permanent shift. It makes it far more interesting and messy and is happening outside the House of Commons. These things haven't happened before in British politics.'

We order another coffee and talk about the negative perception of Jeremy Corbyn that our poll shows and campaigners of all parties have reported from canvassing.

'Jeremy Corbyn has become less of a problem on the doorsteps as the campaign has gone on. He comes across as a decent, honest man and he is all those things. He may be wrong, but he is all those things.

'He's probably there [as leader] for as long as he wants. Labour won't plunge into a civil war if the Conservatives win by a small majority. If there's a landslide, all bets are off.'

Will there be another Corbyn visit?

'We honestly don't know. The tight, professional campaign here in Wales is in contrast to that run from Labour HQ in London. As for shadow cabinet visits, with the greatest respect, there's not much point.'

As our conversation comes to an end, I'm given Welsh Labour's next leaflet. It shows a giant pair of shoes stepping heedlessly over a recognisably Welsh landscape and the slogan, 'Don't let the Tories trample over Wales.' Labour fears its problem will be getting its vote out and hopes this will help.

What about those Labour Leave voters? How big a worry is it that having broken the link with the party they might be prepared to consider voting Conservative?

'We thought leaving the EU would be the big issue and we lined up Labour councillors and supporters who'd voted Leave ready to address that. But we didn't need them. There are two types of UKIP voters. Those who were ex-Tories are going back to the Tories. The working class UKIP voters – most of them are coming back to Labour. Not all of them but most of them. We're not picking up many straight switchers.'

I'm still mulling over all this when I return to Cardiff Bay and bump into Professor Laura McAllister. She says, 'I never bought the idea of a Labour collapse. They're very resilient. They could lose five seats and would still have twenty. The result could still be good for them and good for the Conservatives. Plaid is coming close in Ynys Môn but it's a mistake to talk up seven seats. Coming a good second in Valleys seats will be really good for them.'

Assembly security staff are still checking passes outside the assembly as well as the usual barrier checks inside.

A silence is held for the victims of the Manchester attacks. Politicians and staff stand in public areas of the Senedd while those in committees pause their work.

With Rhodri Morgan's funeral next week, an Assembly official that I chat to in a corridor tells me how strange it is to be organising a funeral in the Senedd, not just a memorial service, but also a family funeral.

I've left my car at home again today so I'm on the train when I hear about a security situation. There were police officers on the train and they're visible everywhere in Newport. No traffic is moving. I walk into town to see large crowds of people standing around, looking for answers. I find my colleagues James Crichton-Smith and Joe Williams in the centre of town and offer to help. James is about to do a Facebook live so I hold his phone for him and then I watch their bags while James and Joe film interviews. One person tells me their car is stuck in the car park and he's been told he can't take it till tomorrow. The owners of one of my favourite cafés, Bar Piazza, come past and say that they were told to leave at 3.30, given no clues about what was happening, just told to close up and clear out.

We walk up to Old Green Roundabout. It's eerie seeing it completely empty of traffic in broad daylight. We're told that all the bridges are closed. Since I live on the other side of the river that means I'm not going anywhere for a while and resign myself to waiting, helping the others and getting sunburnt on one of the hottest days of the year so far. A colleague back in the office tells me to download the We Transfer video sharing app and I pass some of the time recording video of the empty roundabout, the uneasy crowd and a police officer with a sniffer dog.

There's mostly a sort of bemused patience although some people are oblivious to what's happening as they walk determined and head-down. Oblivious then confused when a police officer halts their progress and explains why. Other people are worried. One woman is gesturing at her young daughter as she yells to the police officer, 'But how am I going to get her home?'

We're moved away from the King's Head area, away from its windows. Are they really that worried about an explosion, even a controlled one?

Another colleague arrives and the three of them concentrate on recording interviews for our news coverage. They don't need me as a runner anymore and the lockdown is being eased slightly so that buses are being allowed out and are taking people on board for free. I fight my way through the crowds and hop on one. It's not quite the evacuation from Saigon although it feels very much out of the ordinary. The bus heads in a circuitous direction but it passes near enough to where I live for me to get out and walk the rest of the way home. I'm left thinking how this has been the second time in two months that I've been caught behind a police cordon while a security alert unfolds. Even stranger for it to have happened in Newport.

'This is bonkers...'

Soon after the election, one of the Conservative MPs to make it back to Westminster described it to me as the worst campaign they'd ever been involved in. The manifesto it seems was just one of the self-inflicted problems with the Conservative campaign.

'We hadn't had time to prepare,' I was told. 'The manifesto was clearly put together in a hurry, self-evidently because it fell apart in a hurry too. We had not only bad election materials, printed materials, we actually had a lack of printed materials to the extent that we spent the entire campaign essentially relying on one printed document.'

Not just that but I've heard repeated complaints about major failings in targeting and canvassing. An experienced campaigner was astonished when they helped out in a target constituency to find canvassers not knocking on every door in a street but only going to houses recorded as 'Labour waverer households.'

My source said, 'You get a sort of feel for a street and you look at it and you think this is probably going to have quite a few Tories in… So we were walking down this street, wearing our rosettes, and people were standing in their gardens who looked very likely households for us and you could see they were wondering 'Why are these people walking past us?"

After getting too many people saying, 'I'm Labour and I've always been Labour' my contact asked to look at what the canvassers were working from.

'Sure enough these people were recorded as Labour waverers but the last canvas was dated 2008. So I said, 'This is bonkers. You've really got to stop this' but they said they'd been told to use it and if they don't they will have their central office funding taken away from them. I said this is bonkers. They stopped doing it and central office didn't take any money away. But it seemed to be to be based on a lot of misapprehensions.'

That complaint is completely rejected by someone close to the top of the Tory campaign in Wales.

'I think that the complaints were more about geography and the transportation issues, i.e. you're getting in a car, driving to one house and then driving back. Whereas the old style campaigning involved just knocking every door.

'In 2015 it worked beautifully. There was no reason to believe it wouldn't work in 2017 and in fact it did happen again: we were targeting the right people.

'We picked up votes in thirty-nine out of the forty seats and the houses we went to were responsive. They were people coming over to us.

'It's a fine line. If it wasn't for the collapse in the Lib Dems and UKIP, your first poll could have been about right.'

This election will prove fertile ground to academics and to other political parties. A Labour figure said to me, 'I think it's fair to say the one thing no political party will do after the election is to look at how the Tories ran their campaign and take any leaves out of their book.'

FRIDAY 26TH MAY

Somebody in the Welsh Government tells me they've heard there were two causes of the security incident in Newport. One was a hire car with a gas canister and wires visible. Police couldn't trace the owner so had to destroy it. The other was a backpack that had been dropped by a child with a teddy bear and a iphone charger. Nothing has been publicly confirmed by the police.

Talking of security, I pass a large group of security staff and armed police officers at the entrance to the Assembly car park. They seem to be watching a demonstration of someone in a suit checking beneath a car with a long pole of the kind used to examine for bombs. I'm asked for my building pass as well as my car park pass but one armed officer chuckles as I drive past, 'Ah, we don't know you!'

The BBC still don't know who the Conservative will be for their debate because Andrew RT Davies has pulled out and Alun Cairns is refusing to do it. There's obviously a problem of some kind behind the scenes because Radio 4's Any Questions, which is in Wales, was trailed this morning, naming the whole panel but without a Conservative.

A quick interview with Carwyn Jones outside Transport House. He says it's been a strange week but thinks it's time to restart campaigning. I ask him about the controversy over Jeremy Corbyn's decision to blame the causes of terrorism on some British foreign policy. He refuses to criticise the UK leader but I think that criticism, of his timing at least, is implicit in what he says.

'Well we always have to look at the reasons for terrorism but what we're dealing with here is a group of people who can't be negotiated with.'

When I push him, he says, 'I think these are issues that we have to deal with in time. The priority at the moment has to be to assist the police in their investigation.'

Chatting afterwards, I mention that we have another poll next week. One of the First Minister's advisers jokes, 'Yeah, you need to stop doing those now; they've stopped being helpful.'

The Welsh Liberal Democrats launch their Welsh manifesto with the help of Nick Clegg. They choose to launch in Hay-on-Wye which is in one of their target constituencies, Brecon and Radnorshire, but a more pressing reason may have been that their former leader was at the Hay festival promoting his book.

UKIP launches its Welsh manifesto. In Owain's report, gone are the flags and huge crowds of referendum rallies. Instead just a handful of members and a few journalists attend the small event in Cardiff Bay.

I go through some of the seats which could change hands with a senior Labour person who describes Bridgend and all the Northern seats as 'difficult' and Ynys Môn as 'impossible to tell.'

The party was concerned about Cardiff South and Penarth at the beginning but is less worried now; similarly Cardiff Central. we were slightly concerned at the first poll. They're 'not picking up any momentum' for Plaid in Llanelli or Rhondda. Gower is 'possible' but would be a surprise.

I chat to a senior Conservative AM who tells me they always thought winning twenty-one seats was 'fanciful.' Their prediction: 'A rugby team and a few reserves.' But they say, 'We're doing it on a rising vote, not like 1983 when Labour's vote was split. It must worry Labour. Something has shifted. Theresa May's had a few knocks but is still well liked on the doorstep.'

On air I say how what happened Monday night has completely changed an already extraordinary campaign. I describe the parties as unsure and lacking momentum, a little bewildered.

'...The First Sign This Was a Generational Election.'

There's no doubt Labour won the social media war, but was it luck or strategy? Soon after the election, an AM I bumped into in a restaurant told me something that I've heard several times since: that, yes, social media played the biggest role it had played in a campaign yet and that, 'We didn't need to spend much on advertising on Facebook because people were doing it themselves.'

That makes those running the campaign cross. People may have been taking it upon themselves to share posts but the party was far from inactive on the social media front. Welsh Labour had a digital officer and a social media campaign was run from Transport House in Cardiff. They made a great deal of use of a tool developed by the party centrally called Promote which allowed them to target specific voters on Facebook. An official told me, 'As well as Facebook we had pre-roll content on YouTube and we had a lot going on on Snapchat where Jeremy had a really big following. We did lots of social media from Welsh Labour. Obviously candidates did their own as well but we had a targeted social media campaign. I think it was important. The party's Promote tool is generally seen as a massive incredibly useful thing allowing you to target people and particularly young people.'

Perhaps the best analysis of what Labour got right comes from its opponents who are all too aware of being left standing. In 2015 the Conservatives were seen as those who got social media right. Like so much else though, that aspect of their campaign remained unchanged in 2017 despite a transformed online landscape.

At the Conservative conference in Manchester in October 2017, I heard a rueful and admiring presentation from Jamie Wallis, who's Deputy Chair of the Conservative party in Wales but who also runs a social media marketing company and has spent a lot of time analysing what happened on social media during the election campaign.

He found that pro-Corbyn, anti-government campaigners were not only active online but also showed a real grasp of the way that social media works in 2017 and the way that young people in particular use it more often to influence others rather than simply to share messages.

Often they were sharing articles that derided Jeremy Corbyn, but they did so in order to add their views attacking the message of those articles. That was repeated so much that by the time any message was seen by impartial or undecided individuals it was more often than not presented as inaccurate or unreliable and most frequently as a personal attack on Corbyn himself which only served to endear him more to young people.

In other words party messages were often 'polluted and diluted' by the time that undecided voters saw them. Wallis said that was as if every time a volunteer delivered a leaflet it was 'accompanied by a hundred opposition supporters voicing their opinion on every aspect of it.'

Not only was there a willingness to share content that should have been damaging to their own case, to turn negatives into positives, but there was also a seemingly unerring instinct for when to be active online.

Wallis analysed the times when Facebook advertising costs rose and fell during the campaign because its prices increase at times when (mostly) young people are not just online and consuming content but active and engaging with each other. He found that pro-Corbyn, anti-government activity 'almost precisely matched an immediate jump in high levels of engagement for the under thirties.'

In other words, 'Those seeking to spread anti-government messages during the election campaign were highly accurate at picking the right times to begin their activities.'

And they didn't confine themselves to one platform. They were active on many other platforms other than Facebook, such as Instagram and Snapchat.

What is clear is that, as a senior figure on Labour's left told me, 'Social media came into its own. That was behind a lot of the big rallies. Take for instance Whitchurch (Corbyn's rally at the start of the campaign). People were notified via social media only the day before and two to three thousand turned up, a huge number of them young people. Cardiff was the first sign that this was a generational election.'

MONDAY 29TH MAY

I hear that the stand-off over who will represent the Conservatives in the BBC Wales debate has been resolved. Their education spokesperson in the Assembly, Darren Millar, will do it. That's unexpected. I wonder what the row was that led to that decision.

We receive a press note saying that Carwyn Jones will be campaigning in Torfaen, Newport West and Cardiff South and Penarth, all of which have been strongly Labour seats. Is that a sign of worry and that those areas need extra support?

TUESDAY 30TH MAY

Ahead of tonight's debate on BBC Wales, the differences within the Conservatives have spilled out and become a story, now that it's been confirmed that neither Andrew RT Davies nor Alun Cairns will represent the party. Instead it'll be Darren Millar.

Vince tells me that the original bid from the BBC went, as ours did, to Alun Cairns, and after some toing and froing, it was agreed that Andrew should do it and the BBC's Ask the Leader programme because he'd done ours and there was a feeling there should be continuity of representative in all three programmes. So he booked new flights to come back in the middle of his anniversary holiday. Then it was decided that Alun would do Ask the Leader in Wrexham, breaking the agreement so Andrew decided not to come back for the BBC debate. 'There's been no falling out but he's not going to reschedule his whole life and I don't think his wife was too impressed that he was interrupting their anniversary anyway. Darren will be great. In any case Andrew is quite calm about it. The press interest is ludicrous.'

Owain gets the official statement:

With the Secretary of State unwilling to take part in the General Election debates, Andrew was more than happy to fill in – but that agreement was reached on the basis that it would be best for the party to put forward one candidate for all of the programmes.

Given that Alun was willing to take part in the Ask the Leader programmes Andrew felt that it was no longer necessary to return from celebrating his wedding anniversary to do the debate. It's a bit of a surprise that Alun isn't taking part tonight, but our Policy Director Darren will do a brilliant job.

A Conservative I speak to is much more critical, saying, 'He [Alun Cairns] refused it. It looks like he bottled it. I don't know why he doesn't want to do it. As for this spurious explanation (about not having Assembly members involved) the precedent was set by Cameron who pushed for Leanne to be involved in 2015. Anyway Ruth Davidson is doing it in Scotland. And if it has to be parliamentary candidates, why no opposition to Darren doing it? It's an unforced error. It must be about protecting Alun from taking part in the debate.'

Alun Cairns tells Jeremy Vine on Radio 2 that he was 'never' going to take part in the programme and that it was 'always intended' that Andrew RT Davies would represent the party.

A source close to the Welsh Secretary tells us that since Mr Davies wasn't available, it was 'always the plan' for Mr Millar to represent the Conservatives. The same source highlighted the fact that the Labour representative is not the Shadow Secretary of State, Christina Rees, but Carwyn Jones who's not standing in this UK General Election.

A very senior Conservative calls from the campaign trail. 'There's a fair amount of concern and bafflement that there's no parliamentary candidate in this debate. Any idea why?' I explained what I knew of the situation and what happened with our debate as well as pointing out that two of the panel are candidates. Are they blaming the BBC? 'No, our side. None of us can understand why it's happened.'

They're still optimistic about the party's chances though. 'I've not noticed any change on the doorsteps. People who loathed Tories say they're thinking of voting for us.'

Security is still tight in Cardiff and questions of security dominate the discussion on Sharp End. There's agreement that with such a major sporting event in Cardiff it's completely appropriate to deploy armed police.

The cost of policing and numbers of officers is a hot topic. Jonathan Edwards wants to see policing devolved. David TC Davies acknowledges reduction in police numbers but says it's more about empowering those officers.

There's much sharper disagreement between Carolyn Harris and David Davies over Jeremy Corbyn's record of voting on security matters and connections with IRA and other groups. Carolyn repeatedly says, 'He's signed up to the manifesto now,' while David repeatedly replies that 'This is your leader.' Jonathan Edwards distances himself from the others by saying, 'This is why you can't trust either of the two parties because it's always about personal point scoring.'

Eluned Parrott criticises them too: 'At a time like this it's really distasteful to see the political point scoring on this when people are grieving.' Kris Hicks backs a return to internment advocated by Paul Nuttall. Eluned Parrott and Carolyn Harris vehemently disagree, adding that 'that takes me back to 1939.'

I ask David Davies about tonight's TV debate and what's led to neither of the two main Welsh Conservative leaders appearing. He says, 'I don't know the exact reasons but I can tell you there's no row in the Conservative party. These are two men I've been in contact with on an almost daily basis. I count them both as close personal friends. They're friends with each other. There is no row and what's ironic about this is that one minute we're being accused in the Conservative party of relying on one person, Theresa May, and the next we're being accused of having too many people. The reality is we can put up AMs, MPs, we've got a lot of people, we're very happy to put them up before an audience.'

'Top marks for your positivity,' I say, but then read him the official statement.

'I'm not a spokesman so I don't know. My wife would certainly expect me to be there on the anniversary, I can tell you right now. Some things are more important than politics. I was talking to Alun the other day, RT was down at the market with me. They're great guys, great friends with each other, there is no row, we've just got lots of people who we can put up.'

Talking of positivity, Jonathan Edwards says, 'I'm confident Plaid Cymru will have its best ever General Election result on June 8th.'

Amongst other things, we talk about the IFS report which criticises both Labour and Conservative manifestos for being misleading about costings; Tim Farron's faith; tax pledges or otherwise; the idea of a federal UK and legalising cannabis.

It's UKIP's burqa ban proposal that leads to the most explosive exchanges. Against the criticism that it's oppressive for telling women what they can and can't wear, Kris Hicks says the people who are telling women what they can and can't wear are oppressive husbands and fathers.

Carolyn Harris says, 'I can't believe what I'm hearing. Women should be able to wear what they want.' David Davies says he's uncomfortable with a ban but thinks the wearing of burqas should be discouraged by communities themselves. He says, 'There is a problem with women's rights in Muslim communities. Whenever we talk to Muslim community leaders, they seem to be men.'

Eluned Parrott says, 'I'm deeply uncomfortable with a row of white men telling Muslim women what they can and can't wear.'

They may have been sharp exchanges on air but off-air some of them clearly quite like each other. Carolyn and Jonathan both serve under David TC Davies' chairmanship of the Welsh Affairs Select Committee. Jonathan teases David that he should be leader. Carolyn reveals that she and David Davies have gone salsa dancing together.

When we're testing microphones I often ask guests something trivial, what they've eaten or similar. Tonight it's about what they're wearing. Kris Hicks reveals his suit is handmade in India, somewhere he visits a lot because his wife is Indian, while David Davies proudly reveals that his M & S suit cost him £115. Jonathan Edwards doesn't know how much his suit cost but says he's had it for years. Eluned Parrott remarks that she's realised she's dressed entirely in black. While Carolyn Harris reveals that the cardigan she's wearing was given to her by a constituent after she admired it on the doorstep.

'I guess they gambled on the polls being brilliant...'

The Welsh Conservatives added to their troubles in some of the places they really needed to win. The arguments over selections may not have lost them those seats because the Labour surge overwhelmed them anyway. But it did lose them at least the enthusiasm of some previously loyal supporters in some constituencies, chief amongst them Bridgend, Newport West and Delyn.

The motive was clear. As a senior party figure put it to me, 'We've never elected a Welsh Conservative woman and I think we are worse for that. We need more Welsh women in Conservative politics.' That irks some of those on the receiving end of the decision who would have accepted, say, an all-female shortlist but instead were presented with a shortlist of just one.

'I guess they gambled on the polls being brilliant,' said another. When all the evidence pointed to Conservatives winning new seats it was logical that ensuring there were female candidates in those constituencies would achieve that aim without forcing out any of the returning male MPs. It did mean, however, disappointing some long-established local hopefuls in those constituencies.

In Bridgend the local association refused to make a selection and a candidate was chosen centrally. During the election I received anonymous emails from 'a concerned Conservative' to which I refer in the diary section.

In Newport West, Labour's Paul Flynn claimed that some local Tories had told him they'd vote for him after their association was threatened with dissolution if they didn't choose the centrally-approved candidate. That may have overstating the situation; I'm told there was no threat to dissolve the association, rather to impose the candidate as happened in Bridgend.

In Delyn, a local councillor who'd been a candidate in 2016 quit the party in protest. Huw Williams later told the *Denbighshire Free Press* that 'The Welsh party are quite out of touch with what goes on outside Cardiff. There are other reasons, but I feel Cardiff's ruling the nest but they probably haven't visited North Wales and they don't know what the local association members want. The party in Wales, Cardiff especially, the higher-ups are out of touch with the members on the ground.'

The group leader on Denbighshire is quoted as saying, 'It's nothing to do with the Conservative group on the county council, he has decided to resign from the Conservative Party over the issue with the Parliamentary election, that's all I really know.'

One Tory said to me, 'I was told 'they're picking their future colleagues' and there was a lot of people behind the scenes trying to get X into a certain seat or Y into a certain seat and actually all it served to do was alienate the voluntary party of what we actually have.'

Another puts it down to 'sheer arrogance. We're doing so well in the polls, we can drop in our friends.'

Not true said another campaigner. They were choosing future cabinet members. With what seemed like a strong chance of winning MPs, those new MPs had to be of the best, rather than those who were popular locally, so trying to stop associations picking THEIR friends.

Whatever the motive, I've been given multiple reports of women being contacted by senior Tories – 'phoned out of the blue' is the *phrase I've heard repeatedly – and asked to consider standing even though they weren't thinking about it.*

Someone who was chosen as a candidate noted that local party members didn't always appreciate what being a candidate involves. 'What hurdles do you have to jump. It's not just a question of a nice interview with an amenable chat. You have to jump through significant hoops. There was sometimes ... a lack of understanding as to what the process is. Then we end up in a situation where you're in an association and you like somebody who says I want to be the candidate. You think, I like you, we get on, you're nice and you come out delivering leaflets on a Saturday morning so I'm going to vote for you. But I don't know how well you're going to deal with media or issues in the house or are you capable of committee work. In all honesty as candidates we don't even know that until you're put in that position, you're on Sharp End and you're asked an awful question but at least the process we're taken through as candidates means that you are tested to some degree as to whether you've got those abilities.'

But in some of the cases, those who were overlooked had been through the same gruelling processes: stringent testing, training, expense and disruption. One of those told me that they weren't expecting to 'walk into' being selected simply because of all that, but had expected a 'competitive selection.' Which they didn't get. Instead they got a phone call, showing 'great empathy', they insist, telling them they hadn't made the shortlist. In fact it was a shortlist of one.

'I was expecting a difficult battle,' the disappointed candidate told me. 'I didn't expect to be blocked.'

Whatever the reasons, the effect was to make loyal supporters simply not help out. 'It did stop people knocking the doors with enthusiasm,' said one. 'They stopped knocking doors altogether,' said another. 'We're not blessed with resources in Newport West or Bridgend but what resources we did have, they were gone because they'd had this imposed candidate.'

Another said, 'Newport West and Bridgend were on the cards. There were some ludicrous ones being mentioned like Cardiff South and Penarth and Cardiff West which we were never going to win, but Newport West and Bridgend were potentially on the cards and you literally just cut away your support network in one fell swoop.'

It also made the task much harder for those selected. 'They were traumatised,' a senior Tory told me long after the election and it seems likely they won't stand again.

One who was selected and branded as an 'imposed' candidate denies that and says the problems were frustrating but were overcome until the Labour surge swept away any serious chance they had. 'It took the shine off what could have been really positive,' they told me, describing what happened as 'a distraction, white noise.'

'What happened certainly didn't help, it didn't win people over. I would say I spoke to maybe half a dozen people on the doorstep who raised it, not considerable numbers, but they raised it, saying, 'Oh, you're the imposed candidate.' I tried to explain how the selection process works but already my cards were marked. I don't think it cost me the election but it certainly didn't help.'

On the other side, one of those who missed out reported a deeper disillusion about what happened, the way it was handled and the way it has been since.

Nick Webb, who'd long been an active campaigner in Newport West and had fought for the seat in 2015 was disappointed to be blocked from standing in 2017 when a shortlist of one was imposed on the local association.

After the election he wrote a long and detailed email to the Welsh Conservative board, calmly setting out his concerns over 3,600 words. I'll quote the last paragraphs:

It is quite apparent to me that a very small number of people had presumed that the party would gain Newport West irrespective of the candidate selected and abused their power by hand picking a candidate rather than allowing the membership of the Association to select from a fair and competitive shortlist.

It is also clear that the approach of people being approached directly having either not expressed an interest in a particular seat or even in standing at the election at all makes a mockery of having a rigorous Parliamentary Assessment Board system.

I have spent more hours and money on helping this party than I care to think about. With the expected boundary changes forthcoming, I did not even think that I would live in a target seat for future elections, yet despite this I carried on working hard for the party locally. When my opportunity looked to have arrived the autocratic approach taken slammed the door in my face. I feel utterly used by a Welsh Conservative Party which no longer seems to share my principles of rewarding hard work with opportunity.

It is difficult to know quite how to conclude this email. There is not really a question I can ask, because there is not really an answer which would put right what has occurred. Then again, this is not an email I ever wished to write and has occurred from a situation which was wholly outside of my control. My relationship with the Welsh Conservative Party has changed but not through my choosing.

The only response he's had to that 3,600 word-email is: 'Dear Nick, Many thanks for this. Kind regards.'

No calls, no emails, no after-care. When I spoke to Nick after the election, he told me, 'It saved me time and money. But the longer-term damage is there. It makes it quite difficult to be enthused by the party. The ongoing silence and the lack of anyone taking responsibility is making it worse.'

WEDNESDAY 31ST MAY

A Cardiff that was jittery last week is on lockdown this week. There are yellow security gates at key points in the streets, concrete barriers, a lot of people in hi-vis jackets and a lot of police officers, some armed. It's unfortunate then that I've lost my train ticket. I show the official my receipt and return ticket in the hope he'll let me through. He looks stern and then says, 'Just jump over, fella.' If I could, I would.

Cardiff Bay is beginning to be transformed for the Champions League events that'll be held here at the weekend. There are stalls, tents and a floating pitch in the bay itself.

When I arrive for the funeral, there are already hundreds of people. Most in the long line which snakes from the Senedd, down its steps and into the bay are politicians or connected with politics, although there are well-wishers among them too. Members of the public who don't want to take up the open invitation to go inside have taken their seats on benches in the sun outside.

145

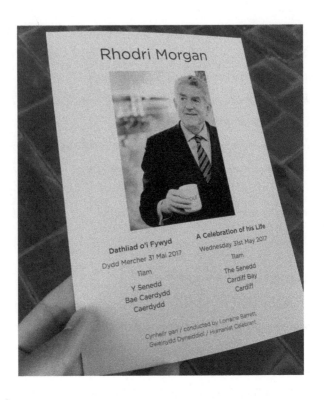

Rhodri Morgan

Dathliad o'i Fywyd
Dydd Mercher 31 Mai 2017

11am

Y Senedd
Bae Caerdydd
Caerdydd

A Celebration of his Life
Wednesday 31st May 2017

11am

The Senedd
Cardiff Bay
Cardiff

Cynhelir gan / conducted by Lorraine Barrett,
Gweinydd Dyneiddiol / Humanist Celebrant

You get the impression Rhodri Morgan has already imprinted his personality on the whole thing: there's laughing, politics being discussed and big political names queuing along with staff members.

I came expecting it to be sombre but the laughter and the chatting – gossipping even – is free and easy. People are tweeting. As I find my place I notice Harriet Harman, Neil Kinnock and Glenys Kinnock in the queue. I note on twitter that 'there's an extraordinary mixture of sadness & public celebration here at the Senedd for Rhodri Morgan's funeral.'

The first person I see is Louise McGee, freshly installed as chief executive of Welsh Labour. I congratulate her. She's talking to Iain McNicol who says that he's here representing UK Labour because Jeremy Corbyn is at an election launch and Gordon Brown couldn't get here.

I ask Alun Cairns about the change in the Tory performance in our poll. He says he doesn't see it on the doorstep. Owen Smith tells me how different this election is for him because he only has to campaign in his own seat. I guess that's one upside to his being out of the shadow cabinet following last year's leadership challenge. The news breaks that Jeremy Corbyn will take part in the final debate after all. I mention this to a senior Labour figure who shrugs and says, 'I don't think it makes any difference.'

Most, three hundred or more, make it into the Senedd, to

standing room if not seats. There's between a hundred and two hundred of us outside, standing, sitting or leaning. Many of those here are tanned from campaigning. MPs such as Owen Smith, Jessica Morden and Chris Bryant are sitting on the steps or perched on railings. The slate walls are as cold and hard as I can attest.

When the family arrives it grows silent. His grandchildren are in Welsh rugby shirts. The coffin is carried past a line-up of Labour staff and MPs.

Lorraine Barrett, the former Assembly Member who's presiding over the ceremony describes Rhodri Morgan as, 'Very much the people's first minister.'

When his grandson Ifan sings *Calon Lân* unaccompanied, there are tears in people's eyes. Then applause. At different points it makes me smile to see the grandsons in their rugby shirts, smiling with recognition at some of the stories, elbowing each other, laughing, occasionally yawning.

Prys Morgan tells how his father gave him the task of teaching his younger brother to speak. The renowned academic calls him, 'Not only my first pupil, my best pupil.' He reveals how the young Rhodri would send jokes to the Beano and Dandy for extra pocket money. 'The best training' says his brother, for becoming First Minister.

His daughter Mari gives a eulogy that has everyone laughing. 'There's been times at the dinner table when you thought, 'Oh God, someone's mentioned the Cuban Missile Crisis. We'll be here for hours!"

She recounts how others at school would say to her, 'I saw your dad on the telly last night, he was wearing odd socks. His appearance as First Minister was a miracle.'

'Maybe he was the father of devolution, I don't know, or the father of the nation. But what I do know is that first and foremost and always he was our father and later their grandfather and we're going to miss him hugely.'

His successor as First Minister, Carwyn Jones, recites Dylan Thomas' poem, 'Do Not Go Gentle' into that good night. As he steps away from the lectern, he touches the coffin.

There's music as well as tributes. There's jazz music and applause as the coffin is borne on the shoulders of family members, the applause rippling out of the Senedd and into the bay as the coffin makes its way into the crowd. It intensifies as the hearse leaves and then I notice that Julie and her family are sharing tears and hugs in the midst of this large, public event.

I stop Stephen and Glenys Kinnock to film their reaction. Glenys says, 'I feel very emotional. He was a dear, dear friend. I can hardly believe that we won't have ever again that kind of joy.'

Harriet Harman is in a rush to catch her train but she pauses to give me her thoughts: 'He was a very unusual politician because he showed you could be an incredibly powerful leader but also a gentle person.'

We broadcast Lynn's lovely interview with Julie Morgan who talks of their strong political and personal partnership. She tells Lynn how their dog Tell is bereft at the loss of his constant walking companion. When we recorded the Welsh Bites programme with him, I asked why his dog was called 'Tell.' It's short for William Tell, Rhodri told me, because when his father was young his grandfather had a dog called William Tell and so it became a family name. And why William Tell? 'Oh, I've no idea.'

On air I say that, 'He was one of the most significant people in the history of Welsh politics. No ifs no buts.' I talk about how he was one of the first politicians I had any serious dealings with, how he'd make time to give comments and to pass on stories. I note that those tangents he was renowned for could make him infuriating to interview. And I end by saying, 'He wasn't the only founder of devolution, but he was the father of devolution. I don't think anyone will challenge him for that title.'

THURSDAY 1ST JUNE

The Champions League Final means that Cardiff Bay is closed to traffic so I get the train and walk down deserted roads into a central area that's already thronging with people. A giant replica of the Champions' League cup stands at the roundabout opposite the Wales Millennium Centre.

With just a week to go, our penultimate poll is published. Roger's article for our website sums it up thus:

The revival in the fortunes of the Welsh Labour party is holding firm, while Plaid Cymru and the Liberal Democrats are on course for historically bad election results.

Labour's support is now at 46%, that of the Conservatives is at 35%. Plaid is at 8%, the Liberal Democrats are at 5% and so is UKIP. Roger's seat projection gives Labour twenty-seven seats, the Conservatives nine, Plaid Cymru three and the Lib Dems one.

Someone I know in Jeremy Corbyn's team messages me about the poll: 'So Labour up to an eleven point lead. Blimey!' I ask if it chimes with what they're finding. 'It chimes. But the big question is the weighting for the youth vote.'

Then a Welsh Labour source texts on the same subject of the lead. 'Purely between us – it's far bigger than it should be, I think, and very soft. That's my gut. But does feel like we're ahead and it chimes with a genuine and warm response to our campaign – and says that our decision to differentiate and also to hammer the Tories was right call.'

As Nick notes, it's clear there is a Labour lead in Wales but also that Labour now has to work for its vote, even in areas where it had traditionally overwhelming support. People are persuadable but can't be taken for granted.

A Conservative source tells me it seems clear the first poll was an outlier. Does this one chime? 'Yes, twenty seats was always mad. A good night will be if we come back with a couple of extra seats: Wrexham Bridgend, Newport West. Labour are still defending.'

Neil Hamilton walks past us in the Assembly canteen and jokes, 'Theresa May's doing very well, isn't she?'

Owain has spoken to a very senior Plaid Cymru person about Llanelli and it's clear they're no longer considering winning there.

They tell him that, 'Nia is very hardworking and Mari is a first-time candidate' which sounds like a pre-emptive defence.[25]

I talk to a Labour contact on Anglesey who fills me in on the picture in that least predictable of constituencies. 'I've heard people saying that Albert has forgotten his grassroots.[26] Ieuan is very well liked and hasn't been away even though he's been out of office.[27] He's always buying his shopping in Llangefni. People have always seen him there. If Michelle had stood again she could have won it for the Conservatives.[28] UKIP seem to be dead on the island.'

I speak to the Labour AM Dave Rees who reports changes in the response on the doorsteps.[29] Some traditional Labour voters are still saying 'no' to the party under Corbyn but others – new voters – are saying yes. He ends by telling me to keep my eye on Gower. 'If we get our vote out, it's one to watch.'

On air I say that our poll shows that Labour's fight back is holding here in Wales and that two-party politics are squeezing the others. But I note that it doesn't take into account what's happening on the ground and on that front Labour still think they might lose a couple of seats while Plaid Cymru are still optimistic they will gain some.

---

[25] Nia Griffith, the sitting MP for Llanelli; Mari Arthur, Plaid Cymru's candidate for Llanelli in 2017
[26] Albert Owen, the sitting MP for Ynys Môn
[27] Ieuan Wyn Jones, former MP and AM for Ynys Mon, former Plaid Cymru leader who was standing again in 2017
[28] Michelle Willis who stood for the Conservatives in 2015
[29] Labour AM for Aberavon

I also note that young voters are overwhelmingly telling us they'll vote for Labour, if Labour can persuade them to vote.

I want to get a sense of another constituency that defies national polling, Ceredigion. Gethin James was a UKIP candidate in 2015 and an Independent councillor until May. I've always found him very clear-eyed about politics, including his own prospects but now that he doesn't have a vested interest, I imagine he'll be interesting to talk to. I'm right. He tells me how the Lib Dems are making, as expected, a huge and visible effort to keep Mark Williams. He's seen and heard a lot about the Plaid candidate, Ben Lake and has seen some Labour campaigning. The UKIP candidate, he describes as a paper candidate – he works in Neil Hamilton's office, lives in Cardiff and doesn't drive.

Then comes the shock. He tells me, 'I think I'm voting for Plaid Cymru.' He explains: 'Only one of two people are going to win in Ceredigion and such is the anti-Brexit stance from the Liberals, I want to silence the Liberals. You can't negotiate if Brussels know there'll be another referendum. So looking at it cold and hard, where is my vote going to be most effective? I'm never going to get someone who shares my vote but I might be able to silence the Liberals.'

Might others follow his example? 'Eighteen thousand people voted Leave in Ceredigion, why would you vote Liberal if you voted Leave? What's more Plaid have chosen well in choosing Ben Lake, a young guy with no baggage – what has anyone got to knock him for? And they've said they want to get the best Brexit for Wales, which is close to what I campaigned for.'

He also thinks there might be some disgruntled Conservatives looking for a home for their vote in what he describes as another case of a 'candidate brought in from Westminster.'

Gethin continues, 'Had we spoken six weeks ago, and had the Conservatives chosen a good local candidate, we could have been looking at an increased Tory vote and I might have considered voting differently. As it is I will have to put a peg on my nose when I vote Plaid. And if people like me are thinking about voting Plaid Cymru, Ceredigion has got a chance of changing.'

This gives me much pause for thought.

SUNDAY 4TH JUNE

I'm doing a live insert into our Sunday programme, Newsweek Wales, from my home. Howard the cameraman arrives and starts trailing cables across the room while I make us tea. The dog is curious about it all. The production staff in the Cardiff gallery are more interested in seeing the dog on camera than me.

Of course, everything's changed because of the terrorist attack on London Bridge. This segment had been planned weeks ago as a chance to take stock of the campaign and look forward to the final few days. But on Saturday night, news started coming through of the terrible events at London Bridge. The Newsweek team had spent all morning changing their programme and my contribution was different too. I talk about the suspension of campaigning – now the third time it's been suspended here in Wales – the calls for the election to be postponed and responses from Carwyn Jones, Leanne Wood and others.

Regarding the campaign itself, I report that Conservatives are saying they never thought they'd win a landslide or even a majority of seats in Wales but think they're still on course to make gains. Privately Labour still expect to lose some seats in Wales and that the Conservatives will win a majority UK-wide. I add that people in other parties think Plaid Cymru could still spring a surprise in one, two, or three seats. I also say it looks like being a difficult election for the Lib Dems and that support for UKIP seems to be evaporating. I end by saying that what happens on Thursday is anybody's guess.

Then I make us another cup of tea.

MONDAY 5TH JUNE

We meet to discuss our overnight election coverage, including which counts we should be at with reporters, cameras and which means to use to feed the material back to Assembly Square. The combined count for Cardiff North, West and Central is where I'll be for the ITV network overnight programme. We also plan to be at the counts for Ynys Môn, Ceredigion, Vale of Glamorgan, Rhondda and the joint counts for Gower, Swansea East and West, Delyn & Alyn and Deeside, Bridgend and Ogmore, Wrexham and Clwyd South, Newport East & West and Neath & Aberavon. We discuss what we'll do about Vale of Clwyd, Blaenau Gwent and Carmarthen East. Nick is getting anxious about those.

During the meeting, Nathan Gill, UKIP MEP and Independent AM texts with sad news: 'Sorry to have to inform you Sam passed away at 10am this morning.'

Sam Gould who worked for Nathan, was a familiar face to everyone who worked in Welsh politics. He stood as a candidate in Caerphilly in 2015 and made a name for himself with good-hearted stunts that sometimes backfired, most notably when he wrote, 'We Love Nige' in the sand at Margate beach. The tide suddenly came in, trapping him, and photos of him being hauled up the sea wall made the papers and Have I Got News For You.

It was he who'd come up with the idea of a purple bus in that campaign and had projected a huge UKIP logo onto Caerphilly Castle. He'd always stop and talk and was pretty much always smiling. A very likeable man. Some UKIP people can be accused of wanting to turn the clock back on a whole range of social issues;

he just wanted out of the EU. He was only thirty-three and had bowel cancer.

An obviously upset Llŷr Powell tells me he only saw Sam last Thursday. 'He was in agony but got up to go to his daughters' school. They and their classmates had made cupcakes for him and he wanted to surprise them.'

Llŷr jokes that 'UKIP's campaign this time is boring: no stunts, no purple van, no projections onto Caerphilly Castle or writing 'Farage' in the sand.'

He says they asked Caroline, Sam's wife, whether she wanted them to announce it or not and she said, 'Make a fuss – it's what he'd want. I've just spoken to Haydn who makes our videos and found out that Sam made a video last week for his funeral. He told Haydn, 'It's my funeral, I'm going to be there.''

I share a table at lunch with a Labour AM who, like every other politician whom I ask, 'How's it going?' has no idea but repeats what others have said, that, 'White working class men aren't voting for Corbyn and the security situation doesn't help.'

But there's been a change elsewhere: 'At the start, I had good Labour friends who couldn't stand Corbyn. Now they think he's great. We have a great manifesto. Labour people really like it.'

There's a sense too that things have shifted within the party when it comes to its treatment of Welsh Labour. 'Carwyn played a blinder on the manifesto. He was in the room [at the Clause V meeting] which is why they said yes to devolution of policing. It's there now. So is Barnett Formula reform.'

I text Paul Flynn to see if he's more upbeat about his prospects than he was when he made his 'toast' quip. He replies: 'More optimistic now. There is a favourable Welsh dimension because of Carwyn and memories of Rhodri. Polls have persuaded bookies. Imposing the Cardiff Tory has delivered some disillusioned Tory votes for me.[30] Soft Plaid and Green votes are coming my way but UKIP votes are going to Tories. Corbyn fear is reducing with his TV appearances. Believe Newport seats will stay red.'

A senior Conservative source tells Owain that Clwyd South and Wrexham are still looking good for them while Bridgend and Newport West are 'touch and go'. There'll be a couple of surprises though, the source promises. In another conversation, Owain is told by a senior Lib Dem that they've, 'ploughed a hell of a lot of money into Cardiff Central' but that it doesn't look like they'll now win it.

On the news this evening I remark that another pause has changed an election campaign that's already changed and changed again. How it's disrupted the tone as well as rhythm of the campaign and how it's become about more than just Brexit. I say again that Labour privately still think they'll lose a few seats here and that the Conservatives will win an overall majority.

Theresa May has been in the news saying there's been, 'too much tolerance of extremism' but on Sharp End the non-Tory panellists think that if there has, then as the former Home Secretary, she

---

[30] Angela Jones Evans, the Conservative candidate, was actually from Newport although there was a row over her selection.

should bear some of the blame. The Conservative Byron Davies won't blame her but says, 'Government has to have a new look at the way we deal with it.'

I'm surprised that, as a former police officer, he's not convinced by calls for more officers, but he insists the problem is more about intelligence gathering than numbers. 'If you had twenty thousand extra police officers on the streets of London that night, would it have made a difference? I doubt it very much indeed.'

The others on the panel agree that Theresa May has questions to answer after being Home Secretary for six years. But Joe Smyth says his fellow UKIP member, Suzanne Evans has gone too far by saying Theresa May bears some of the responsibility for what happened.

I ask him about Paul Nuttall's call for a return to internment. 'It didn't work for the conflicts in Northern Ireland. But people come from Syria who've probably committed atrocities and seen what's going on. Once they come into this country then I think they should be held, questioned to see what they've done. We've got good intelligence out there but we can't just let people come from Syria, the atrocities they're committing over there, and let them walk on our streets. It is very difficult but we have to do something.'

Kirsty Williams says there's been a shift in the campaign: 'There was a definite change on the doorstep as soon as the Conservative manifesto was launched.' Byron Davies acknowledges that, 'Some people were concerned about some of the issues' in the manifesto.

There's widespread agreement that politics has polarised. Kirsty

Williams says the other parties are being squeezed by the polarised campaign. UKIP's Joe Smyth agrees that they're being 'squashed' as does Plaid Cymru's Rhun ap Iorwerth although he says that, 'In those seats where we're challenging it's very interesting; our internal polling I can assure you is radically different to the polls we're seeing elsewhere.'

We discuss TV debates. Byron Davies says he didn't even watch our debate which seems harsh. He makes a now familiar jibe: 'I'd be quite interested to see in the next Assembly election if we have a panel of MPs debating.' [31]

I say to him, 'You have a word with your party but since you've raised this sensitive topic why wasn't Andrew RT Davies involved, why wasn't Alun Cairns?'

He won't bite. 'You'll have to ask them. I think they had some arrangement. I haven't entered into it. I've been far too busy knocking doors to get involved in media tussles.'

Exasperated, I say, 'Ah, it's not media tussles, it's you lot.'

Joe Smyth says some of his UKIP friends are considering voting Conservative just to stop Labour. I ask him if he thinks they'll have any MPs and he says, 'I don't know.' I tell him I like his honesty.

After the programme I ask Byron Davies if he thinks he's safe in Gower. Of course he says 'yes,' but I'm sure I can read a bit of

---

[31] For the record, neither panels for our debate nor BBC Wales' consisted of purely AMs as a number of Conservatives were saying. Two of the five were candidates in this election. We invited the parties to nominate their representatives.

uncertainty into his reply. Joe Smyth tells him, 'I'll have a word with the guys down there. Make sure you're okay.' Byron laughs and says, 'I'm glad I came on this programme now.'

Rhun ap Iorwerth tells me that, as a former paratrooper, Joe told him he'd done his homework on his opponents and had watched YouTube videos of all of them, noting that, 'You're the most adversarial.'

I ask Rhun about Ynys Môn and he seems hopeful of Ieuan Wyn Jones' chances. 'He's re-energised. You can never tell though with the island. The numbers are good and people value people who live there and invest in the local area.'

TUESDAY 6TH JUNE

Theresa May is making visits in the North and South. Her name is attached to a second article for the Western Mail in which she says, *Welsh Labour has been trying to shield itself from toxic party leader Jeremy Corbyn throughout this campaign.*

It's clear that the Conservatives continue to see their best chance lies in playing up apparent concerns about Jeremy Corbyn and in Wales trying to demolish the 'Welsh Labour' strategy.

On a farm at Bangor-on-Dee, my colleague Carole Green asks the Prime Minister, 'What's gone wrong with your campaign?' She simply denies that anything has gone wrong. When Carole asks her about Tory infighting she'll only talk about Labour infighting. As for whether or not there's any infighting in her party, all I'll say is that there was no Welsh leader alongside her to comment.

A Plaid person texts about Gower: 'Byron definitely seems rattled from what I've seen.'

I talk to senior members of Welsh Labour's campaign team who tell me that things have changed from the dire situation predicted by our first couple of polls. 'We're in a very different position now,' says one, 'but we're not doing the can-can on the basis of more recent polls.' They confirm that they're still worried about all of the North Wales seats, Newport West and Bridgend.

'The Tories were bullish at the start of the campaign,' says one. Ten extra seats for them was a bit much but was reflective of the situation. Seats they talked up they're not mentioning now. They've retrenched. Carwyn Jones said the political weather was challenging. It feels more clement now. It feels like there are contests everywhere.'

They're also more confident about Blaenau Gwent than they were at the beginning and as for Rhondda: 'Plaid are throwing everything but the kitchen sink at Rhondda. So are we.'

The conversation makes it clear to me that Labour's less pessimistic but still sees this as a defensive election. There's no talk of making gains in Wales but it will rate success as retaining what it already has. They don't think they'll drop as low as our first poll suggested but believe they probably will lose a couple of seats.

What could change things is the support they're picking up amongst eighteen to twenty-four-year-olds but they're not confident they'll turn out in huge numbers.

There's a feeling that despite all the initial gloom, the party has surprised itself as much as anyone else by avoiding the worst case scenario. 'Jeremy has had a really good campaign. Carwyn has had a really good campaign. People are warming to the manifesto, they've responded to it extraordinarily well. Labour supporters in Labour voting areas will vote Labour with greater vigour than before. That's heartening but won't deliver us new seats. I genuinely think Jeremy has proven himself and is someone that people have warmed to.'

I have other conversations throughout the day. A Plaid source tells me, 'Ceredigion is looking quite interesting for us, it looks like the Tory vote will be higher than usual which could squeeze the Lib Dems and Ben is proving very popular in a lot of areas.[32] I think it could come down to what the Corbyn-leaning people in Aber decide to do. In terms of Rhondda, I was feeling very confident a couple of weeks back but Labour seem to have had a real bounce back there over the past week or so and I'm much less confident now.'

Blaenau Gwent? 'I have no idea.'

Ynys Môn? 'I'm fairly confident although as always it's a three party race.'

A phone conversation with a Conservative contact: 'If Labour voters who say they can't stand to vote Corbyn or Abbott move over to us we'll have a good night. Despite Carwyn Jones' best efforts, people are saying to us 'Corbyn' not 'Carwyn.' They keep telling us, 'I can't vote for Corbyn.'

'Gower feels okay. It's almost as if the tougher the area, the better it is. Wrexham, Clwyd South and Newport West feel good.

---

[32] Ben Lake, Plaid Cymru candidate in Ceredigion.

I'm not quite feeling it in Bridgend but others are chipper and canvassing is good. Others are writing off Newport East but it still could be a gain. I'm more positive than I was two days ago but then I'm an optimist.'

I learn that Jeremy Corbyn had a full day of campaigning in Wales planned for last week but it was called off because of the terror attacks. He'll be visiting Clwyd West tomorrow for 'an old-school, whistle-stop' visit.

I have a conversation with a reliable Lib Dem source who tells me, 'We're not expecting to make any gains. It's close in Ceredigion, but we think we will pull through. Decisions made around literature will have hurt us.[33] Tory voters are saying that they lent us their vote previously but will vote Tory this time. We're hoping for an improved showing in those three, narrowing the majorities.'

On air I remark that the London Bridge attack has changed an election campaign that had already changed significantly. The second pause in campaigning at a UK level, the third in Wales has changed the rhythm and the tone, shifting the focus away from Brexit onto security concerns, terror laws and the funding of the anti-terrorist effort.

Jon asks me for my best guess as to the likely outcome and I say, honestly, nobody knows.

----

[33] This refers to a row over a Facebook attack advert accusing Plaid Cymru of backing a 'hard Brexit.' Welsh Lib Dem leader Mark Williams described the ad as 'nonsense' and apologised. The ad was withdrawn.

WEDNESDAY 7TH JUNE

The day begins with a network election night rehearsal beset by glitches but that's what rehearsals are for. The team want to try again and again and I'm in a position to help out, so I spend the day hooked up to talkback, sitting in front of a camera but texting, emailing and swotting up on constituency data. It's fun to listen to George Osborne and Ed Balls settling into their new roles as pundits. They're clearly going to enjoy themselves.

Jeremy Corbyn is making a flying visit to Colwyn Bay. The constituency it's in, Clwyd West, is number one hundred on Labour's list of target seats. It doesn't put off the crowds though – it's estimated more than eight hundred people pack the prom to hear him speak.

Andy Collinson emails to say, 'I have just heard back from Jo Kiernan who has confirmed that Julie Morgan is happy for us to air the modified Bites interview that we did with Rhodri.'

It's time to publish our last poll. As usual, Roger's summary puts it succinctly: 'The final Welsh opinion poll of the 2017 General Election shows Labour on course to maintain their long-standing dominance of electoral politics in Wales. It also shows the Conservatives on the brink of their highest vote share here for more than a century. Both Plaid Cymru and the Liberal Democrats, however, appear to be facing their worst General Election result for many years.'

The figures are: Labour unchanged from the last poll at 46%, Conservatives down slightly again to 34%, Plaid Cymru at 9%, Lib Dems and UKIP both on 5%.

Roger's seat projection suggests that far from losing ten seats, Labour could keep all it has now and pick up two to win twenty-seven. They'd have taken them from the Conservatives who'd hold onto nine seats. Plaid and the Lib Dems would be unchanged, holding onto their three seats and one seat respectively.

A Labour contact texts to say, 'Crikey. For what it's worth, still agree with the direction of that travel. But that lead...'

A senior Labour person in Newport tells me. 'The canvassing returns are much stronger than they were in Newport East. I think Jess will have much the same majority.[34] But the Tories may be operating under the radar. I'm much less positive about Newport West but you can never be sure.'

---

[34] Jessica Morden, the sitting MP for Newport East

I always think the formulation 'so and so whispers to me' is far-fetched but a Welsh Conservative that I speak to in a corridor actually whispers to me when they say, 'I tell you where they're nervous about: Gower.'

My report for Wales at Six features campaigning by leaders of each of the parties with the exception of UKIP whose spokesperson's message is a plaintive, 'Stick with us.' My script says, 'All across the country the political parties have been making themselves as visible as possible in some unlikely places. Unlikely but not impossible in this unpredictable election.'

To illustrate my point, I've filmed at Horton's coffee shop in Newport. I brandish a pile of election leaflets that I've rescued from my own recycling bin. The constituency I live in, Newport East, hasn't seen this much campaigning in a long time – a sign that nowhere is off-limits.

In the Wales at Six studio I describe the poll as good news for Labour but good news too for the Conservatives because while they may have lost their lead, their share of vote is still higher than it's been for a century. It's not so good for the other parties though because they're being squeezed out by the Labour-Tory battle. I remark that something has changed in this election and make a final point that the votes of young people are going to be very important.

'They could ride both horses quite successfully...'

Whether or not it was the 'Welsh Labour' brand and strategy that turned things around for the party in Wales or the Corbyn surge and influx of new voters is a matter of heated discussion.

Since the election some Corbynistas have bridled at analysis that credits a 'uniquely Welsh' campaign built around Carwyn Jones coupled with a surprise surge in support for Jeremy Corbyn and the politics he represents. They've pointed to packed party meetings filled with hundreds of new activists who were knocking doors, posting on Facebook and enthusing others who are also new to voting. They say that enthusiasm sprang from Jeremy Corbyn's leadership and was happening from the start of the campaign.

Labour's opponents have mixed views. One Conservative MP I spoke to was clear that it was Corbyn. 'Carwyn didn't resound at all. He had no influence whatever on the campaign and no one ever talked about Carwyn Jones on the doorstep. Our vote went up... but Labour did even better and I attribute that to Corbyn.'

However, an Assembly-based Tory had a different view. 'Was it Carwyn or Corbyn? Well, probably it's all overstated but it's a bit of both and the fact is they were able to be uniquely Welsh and when they realised that he was coming through over the last fence, they could ride both horses quite successfully.'

A Conservative activist said to me with admiration, 'I take my hat off to them. Welsh Labour ran an excellent campaign; they used Carwyn as an insulating figure.'

A senior member of the Welsh Labour campaign team is bullish about the work that went into shoring up the vote in Wales before the surge: 'It's always tempting to say, as someone from Welsh Labour Grassroots or Momentum might say, 'Oh look it was all fine in the end wasn't it?' To that I would say, 'Bollocks.' If you start off and you're fucked and you finish and you're not, it is for the birds to suggest that everything that happened in the middle didn't count for anything. It did.'

And what happened in the middle, they say, was a concerted 'Welsh' campaign and manifesto.

'We had the best of both worlds,' said a Labour MP to me recently. 'We benefited from something we didn't expect and that was Jeremy Corbyn having such a pull on young people. That certainly helped us in Cardiff North and elsewhere, but also there's evidence to suggest that we held the working class vote in the Valleys to a far greater extent than in parts of England with the same socio-economic structure such as in the Midlands where we lost seats. One of the reasons for that is that working class people who had reservations about Jeremy and his positions on defence etc. were reassured by Welsh Labour. We benefited from that dual approach.'

Where there's disagreement is when the Corbyn surge began and how Welsh Labour responded to it. Someone from the Corbyn team points to what happened at Whitchurch when hundreds of people turned up as an early sign of what was to come: 'It showed very early on in the campaign that there was a huge interest in Jeremy and Welsh Labour underestimated that all the way through.'

They claim too that there was a reluctance in Wales as there was in parts of England to shift from a purely defensive campaign to offensive. 'It wasn't unreasonable given the small amount of money there was at the start to put it into defensive seats at the beginning. What was a bit of a tussle was getting them to shift and move it to offensive seats when the money started coming in.'

The money referred to was a huge injection of funding from unions and online donations that tripled the amount available. Despite that, a key Corbyn ally was horrified to discover quite late on in the campaign that Cardiff North still had no full time staff even though the signs were there that it was winnable.

Some senior Corbynistas in Wales are convinced that there was a dual approach and that it worked. A Corbyn-supporting AM I spoke to in the days after the election said, 'People who were uncertain about Jeremy liked Carwyn but the more they saw of Jeremy they realised he wasn't a monster.'

It often felt during the campaign that Welsh Labour people like Carwyn Jones were reluctant to talk about Jeremy Corbyn or to feature him prominently in election literature. At the London end of the campaign there was a feeling that, while there was no attempt to block the leader visiting, neither was there much eagerness. Welsh Labour wasn't 'knocking down the door' with invitations, I was told. 'Welsh Labour never really grasped what an asset Jeremy was and while they never asked him to stay away never really asked him to come.'

However those I've spoken to still deny there was an attempt to airbrush the UK leader from the Welsh campaign.

As one official put it, 'Jeremy was there at the beginning at Whitchurch, and bookended the campaign with a visit at the end in

Colwyn Bay. There were a couple of other visits planned that never quite came off. He did the foreword to the manifesto. Basically everywhere you look he was there.'

Another Corbyn-supporting AM told me that MPs' dislike and distrust of their leader helped strengthen the Welsh Labour brand. 'There were MPs happier to be associated with Welsh Labour rather than Corbyn. They thought it would be a whitewash, that was their starting point. So that increased the focus on the Welsh Labour brand, on identity. In many ways it presented an opportunity to create that identity, an opportunity that hadn't been there in the past.' As someone in the Corbyn team puts it, 'They would have done the Welsh Labour thing anyway, whoever was leader of the party but the fact that there was tension between Welsh Labour and Jeremy helped it along.'

By accident, design or both the Welsh Labour strategy was widely supported during the campaign and now looks unlikely to be rolled back. Party constitutional changes meant that Carwyn Jones had official internal recognition as the leader of Labour in Wales, including a seat on the National Executive Committee and a role in the all-important Clause V meeting which signed off the manifesto. It had been a long standing joke that I asked Ed Miliband when Carwyn Jones would get the NEC seat he'd promised during his leadership campaign. He never did during that time but he has now and has shown determination to use it.

ELECTION NIGHT
THURSDAY 8TH JUNE / FRIDAY 9TH JUNE

21.00 I arrive at the Institute of Welsh Sport. There's no pass for me so my hi-tech security pass is hand-written. This cheers me.

Makeshift pass in hand, I make my way upstairs to the gallery that overlooks the sports hall where long tables are already laid out. Three counts will be held here tonight: Cardiff North, Cardiff Central and Cardiff West.

The gallery is narrow and we're already tripping over each other. BBC Wales has occupied one end of it, we've occupied the other. Next to us is Channel 4 and Sky News is between them and the

BBC. Newspaper journalists move around and there are some student journalists too. Everyone wants to know where the power plugs are and what the wifi situation is. I plug into my talkback box and can hear the network programme getting ready to go on air.

Our workspaces are three narrow rows of folding chairs and we make use of them for balancing our computers, cables, camera gear, coats, food and drink and occasionally for sitting on. Our camera along with those of the other broadcasters is trained on the hall where the volunteers, officials, party members and ballot boxes are gathering. All of the cameras are feeding the pictures live.

I'm joined by Richard Morgan who'll gather interviews for our news coverage of the counts that are taking place here, as I could be called on to go live at any moment so have to remain on standby, talkback plugged in and mic on. My role will be to report on what's happening across the whole of Wales. Paul Davies is the field producer for tonight and will liaise with the production team in London.

22.00 The Exit Poll is published. It's sensational news. It predicts that the Conservatives will be the largest party but with three hundred and fourteen seats, twelve short of a majority and fewer than David Cameron won in 2015. Labour will win two hundred and sixty-six seats and the Lib Dems fourteen. Plaid Cymru will be amongst the twenty-two 'others' and the SNP will drop to thirty-four. UKIP will get nothing.[35]

----
[35] It was pretty close. The final results were: Conservatives 318, Labour 262, SNP 35, Lib Dems 12, Others 22 including 4 for Plaid Cymru.

In my earpiece I can hear George Osborne telling Tom Bradby that the news is 'catastrophic' for Theresa May. It'll mean a hung parliament, possibly another General Election soon and who knows what else? Theresa May's resignation? Can she form a coalition? Could Jeremy Corbyn?

22.10 Nick posts an update on our website: 'If tonight's exit poll is accurate and the same swing to Labour is seen across Wales, the party could hope to gain three seats tonight. Both Gower and Vale Of Clwyd, which were lost to the Conservatives in 2015, would be recaptured. Cardiff North is also a vulnerable Tory seat on these figures. However, ITV News polling expert Professor Colin Rawlings has said that Wales could be a 'marginal exception' to the swing from Conservative to Labour.'

22.13 I text a Labour contact for a response to the exit poll. He hasn't seen it yet so I tell him the headlines. He responds with: 'If the last eighteen months taught us anything it's that if you take the electorate for granted, they'll give you a kicking...'

22.30 I text a Plaid contact: 'Hi. Any response to exit poll yet?' They respond, 'Hi. Not taking it for granted but obviously encouraging that our vote seems to be holding up. If accurate then Theresa May's cynical gamble has backfired.'

22.35 Carwyn Jones arrives for interviews. He jokes that, 'Two years ago they told me don't look downbeat. Today they've told me, don't look too happy. So I'm just going to look bewildered which is easy because I am.'

I ask him what he puts it down to. 'The only way I can explain it is that turnout is up amongst young people. I saw a lot of young people voting today.' I ask him if he thinks losses in the North are still likely. 'That was based on the opinion polls from a couple of weeks ago. Opinion polls change.'

22.46 Vince texts me his response: 'This is just a projection at this point and we won't have to wait very long to see if it bears out. The response we have had in Wales has been positive and these exit polls assume a uniform swing so we will have to see how local campaigns affect the result. They were wrong last time – let's wait and see.'

23.14 Professor John Curtice gives hope to the Welsh Tories, giving them a better than 95% chance of winning Wrexham, Delyn, Clwyd South and Alyn and Deeside.

23.21 Another Plaid contact is much more pessimistic: 'Unlikely to make any gains. Corbyn bounce very clear everywhere.'

23.30 I talk to a senior Welsh Conservative official who tells me, 'Gower's gone, so is the Vale of Clwyd and Cardiff North is tight.' He's pessimistic about any gains. Newport West? 'No.' Bridgend? 'Not now. Our saving grace might be in the North.'

He adds that 'Welsh Labour had a brilliant campaign. Ours

was non-existent. There was the Scottish campaign and then the England and Wales campaign. We had attack lines on Carwyn Jones and Leanne Wood and were told not to use them. The debates row was embarrassing. It was a shambles.'

23.33 Another Plaid contact texts: 'Looking like it's going to be another of those nights for us! I'm not expecting any gains, we've been totally squeezed, and I'm a bit worried about Arfon if I'm honest. Looks like Labour have signed up a lot of new voters. That said I think any Labour successes will be down to Corbyn rather than 'Welsh' Labour and the Labour MPs will need to decide whether their loyalties lie with Corbyn or Carwyn. Who knows though – Plaid could be holding the balance of power... a govt of national unity!'

23.41 Plaid source: 'Anglesey's looking pretty shit for us.'

'Don't Tweet!'

The angry statement that I scrawled on hotel notepaper the day after the election only gives a hint of the frustration felt by Welsh Conservatives based in the Assembly about what they saw as being completely marginalised in the campaign.

'There wasn't a Welsh campaign,' said one. 'We were marginalised as an Assembly resource but there was a broader theme of Wales and the story of Wales being ignored by London, that it was an England

and Wales campaign run from London. Meanwhile they let Ruth [Davidson] get on with her own thing.'

They were warned not to compete for TV time with Theresa May and shouldn't even put out press releases on Assembly-related issues 'because anything we did could distract from the message of Theresa May.'

They weren't even allowed to use social media.

'Don't tweet, don't post on facebook. If you look back over that period you'll see how much our content dropped off in that period. In the end we just thought 'fuck it.' If this is going to go one way at least if we're out of it then we're not responsible for it.'

From the other side the argument is that this was a UK General Election. An MP told me, 'I really can't understand why Andrew thinks he's been sidelined because it's not really his pigeon, frankly. He's there to run the Assembly elections and make sure we get a good showing then.'

But that sidelining is 'disrespectful to Andrew and the Assembly group,' an activist told me. 'And to the membership. Of the four people who think they're in charge of the party in Wales, Jonathan Evans, Alun Cairns, Richard Minshull and Andrew RT Davies, Andrew is the only one with a mandate. The way he's treated shows a lack of respect for members who voted for him.'

The Welsh Tories thought they'd settled the arguments over the role of the Welsh leader which have raged since Andrew RT Davies was elected by members in 2011. They'd come into the open during the party's conference in Birmingham in 2012 when an extra seat had to be jammed onto the stage so that Davies could take part in a discussion on the future of the United Kingdom.

Before that there had been briefings and counter briefings about his role. Even the then Prime Minister was dragged into it. When I asked him if he considered Andrew RT Davies as more than just Assembly group leader, David Cameron told me, 'I see Andrew as the leader of the conservatives in Wales. He sits in the Assembly but it's a Welsh-wide responsibility that he's got.'

Clearly those arguments haven't gone away. After the election another senior Tory told me, 'We need to have a designated leader here in Wales. This situation cannot continue. Scotland has a good model. These are discussions to be had.' At the time of writing it seems those discussions aren't happening. When I interviewed Theresa May in Manchester in October 2017, she'd reverted to referring to Davies as the Assembly leader and denying there was any need for a single, identifiable leader in Wales. But then she had other matters on her mind.

FRIDAY 9TH JUNE

00.12 My colleague Ian Edwards tweets rumours from the Arfon count that, 'It's looking close between Labour and Plaid Cymru. This will be a big blow to Plaid Cymru.'

00.14 A Plaid contact texts with surprise news: 'Ceredigion looks like a four-way fight. We're still in it but Labour and Tories have come from nowhere.'

00.15 My colleague Hannah Thomas at the Rhondda count reports that, 'Chris Bryant is looking very comfortable and that Plaid Cymru are conceding they're not going to win it.'

00.17 My colleague Carole Greene reports, 'Growing Labour confidence at Wrexham and Clwyd South counts. Also Delyn.'

00.20 In a Whatsapp message, a Labour source dampens talk of being in contention in Ceredigion straight away. 'Despite what Plaid might be saying, we are definitely not going to win in Ceredigion.'

00.21 Plaid pessimism continues despite Ceredigion optimism in this text: 'Campaign has been almost like a presidential election between two personalities. Dominance of two big parties reflecting it. Tough for us but if we keep three we'll be pleased. Arfon is tight.'

00.40 A senior Labour source uses Whatsapp to try to arrange a phone call. I say that I'm just going on air. 'Bollocks. Sorry. Far more positive about North East Wales.'

On air I tell Tom Bradby that the expected Tory surge in Wales had gone into reverse and the party is now looking at losing even those seats it previously held. I mention the 'Welshness' issue of both campaigns: apparently successful in the case of Labour but not at all in the case of the Conservatives whom I describe as 'livid' at the way they were treated by the UK campaign. I end by saying how bad things are looking for Plaid Cymru and how there will be questions about the future of their leader Leanne Wood.

00.50 The senior Welsh Conservative who'd talked to me earlier about 'saving grace' now texts to say, 'that saving grace isn't going to come off.'

00.52 The Labour phone call happens. 'There's been a remarkable turnaround. North East Wales was looking very bad. But our sampling in Wrexham and Delyn puts us in a very strong position. We're far, far more chipper. And the indications are good for the others. In the South, I'm hearing good things in Newport West and Bridgend. We had genuine concerns but the indications are far more positive. Cardiff North will be tight but they're a very enthusiastic CLP.' What about Ceredigion and Arfon? 'If either of those happens, the count's on me.'

00.57 Plaid source: 'We're holding Carmarthen east.'

00.59 A Labour source in Llanelli messages me on twitter: 'They've [Plaid] come third in Llanelli.'

01.00 Someone at Gower texts: 'Numbers looking good to them – cautiously optimistic but will still be close. Tonia very buoyant.'

01.01 A leading Conservative official comes up, shaking his head. 'We might lose Aberconwy. The Vale of Glamorgan is tighter than we'd like. But it looks like our majorities will go up in Brecon and Radnorshire and Montgomeryshire.'

01.05 Lib Dem: 'From what I'm hearing Ceredigion is a four-way but we've fallen behind in Cardiff and Mont, doing better in Brecon but UKIP vote gone to the Tories.'

01.08 Another Labour source: 'We're not briefing we're going to win Aberconwy! It's close but Tories ahead, talk of recount premature!'

01.25 Cardiff North may not be as tight as Labour thinks. I look down to Craig Williams. He looks up with a sad, sheepish grin. I don't want to shout so I make a thumbs up, thumb down, thumb in the middle gesture. Back to the middle. He inclines his head. Back down. He gives me that same sad grin. I mouth to him, 'Sorry.' I know they know what they're getting themselves into, but it can be brutal.

01.31 Plaid relief: 'We won Arfon by a hundred and three. Labour calling recount.'

01.39 Text: 'Recount Aberconwy.' That's a sign of how bad this night is becoming for the Conservatives.

01.50 I go down onto the counting floor to talk to a senior Cardiff Conservative whose eyes are full of tears. 'It looks so different to five weeks ago in the council elections when we were doing so well in wards in Cardiff North. And this was such a good campaign. Craig is such a good candidate.' I ask them if it's looking close enough for a recount. They just look at me and almost imperceptibly shake their head.

02.04 Lib Dem on Ceredigion: 'Mixed reports, only a hundred or so in it.'

02.05 Labour person on Whatsapp: 'Gower and Cardiff North both very positive. As I'm sure you've heard.'

02.06 A Gower source: 'Looks like 2.5k-3k majority.'

02.15 I text a Plaid Cymru source: 'Any news on Ceredigion?'
   'Still too close to call. Recount territory.'
   'Thanks. Between all four?'
   'Just us and the liberals.'

02.19 A contact in Ceredigion messages: 'Reliable source says it's very close in Ceredigion between Lib Dem and Plaid. Possibly as tight as a hundred votes.'

02.26 I tweet that Conservatives are conceding that Cardiff North will be lost to Labour.

03.05 Ceredigion drama continues. A Plaid source: 'Libs just called a recount. We are a hundred and fifty-ish ahead.'

03.06 Another Plaid source: 'Ceredigion recounting again – we're a hundred and fifty ahead.'

03.07 Plaid: 'Full recount. Will be an hour or so.'

03.33 The Cardiff West result is announced. Kevin Brennan dedicates his win to Rhodri Morgan.

03.44 A Conservative messages me: 'It comes back to the need for a national (Welsh) campaign. Look back at May [council elections] And look at what Ruth has achieved with a Scottish campaign. We haven't had a single Welsh media set piece or a single Welsh press story. We need to combine our unionism with a pride and confidence in the 'Welsh' Conservative message.'

In response to tweet based on that, a former candidate Nick Webb replies: 'Perhaps but selection decisions which alienated activists across key seats in Wales, were made in Wales. Not sufficient to just blame London.'

03.55 I text Paul Flynn: 'So you weren't toast.' He replies: 'It would be a great shame if the trajectory of my promising parliamentary career was interrupted as my best years are ahead.'

03.58 On Whatsapp I ask a Conservative, 'What's going on in Preseli?'

'No real intel. Postal votes need to have been good they say locally. Sounds close but I don't know.'

Then, a couple of minutes later: 'Crabby ahead in recount.'

I talk to an elated Alun Davies who unexpectedly hugs me and says 'Fucking brilliant.[36] She deserves it. She's worked so hard.

---

[36] Welsh government minister and partner of the winning candidate, Anna McMorrin

God knows what we're going to do with the kids – are you up for babysitting?'

I ask him when he noticed it changed. 'Two weeks ago we saw it changing. In Blaenau Gwent Plaid just disappeared so I upped sticks and came down here.[37] We noticed a sea-change mid-way. It could have been the Tory manifesto but I can't believe it was just that.'

A senior Conservative tells me, 'Theresa May will have to go. There'll be some strong looking-into things after this. We might have just won our best share of the vote since the First World War and gone back in terms of seats. Look at the Scottish campaign and their big successes – that's what we should have done.'

04.32 It's still going on in Ceredigion. A Plaid Cymru source texts: 'a hundred and three ahead on the second recount. Third recount called.'

04.47 Another Plaid source: 'I think that under the circumstances it's a good result for us to hold our three, if we win Ceredigion I'll be delighted!'

With all the Cardiff results counted, the sports hall rapidly empties of people, tables, ballot boxes and ballot papers. And me too. Paul and I try and fail to book a taxi but strike lucky when one pulls up at the Institute of Welsh Sport for his break. We relocate first to ITV HQ in Assembly Square for some tea and chocolate and then take the short walk to the front of the Senedd where we're due to be on standby for Good Morning Britain.

---

[37] His constituency which he narrowly held against Plaid Cymru in 2016

06.00 We're sitting under a gazebo in front of the Senedd sheltering from heavy showers and gusts of wind that threaten to take the gazebo away from us. Joggers and cyclists speed past us while we sit in deck chairs. One jogger shouts as he goes past, 'She got what she deserves.' Another stops and asks, 'What's the news?' We tell her it's a hung parliament and she jogs on.

Just after 6am the news from Ceredigion finally comes through – a last twist in Wales that make the difference between a poor performance by Plaid Cymru that would have seen immediate questions asked about Leanne Wood's leadership and instead, relief and a fourth MP.

07.30 Owen Smith walks by on his way to be interviewed down the line. He says 'We're going to face a nightmare time with an unstable partnership between the Conservatives and a very right wing DUP and there'll be another election.'

08.00 A Conservative official: 'We were marginalised and sidelined. We were ready to do the heavy lifting but they let us do nothing. We weren't allowed a single press release. We were fucked over and it's a shower of shit.'

08.45 It seems the signs were there for the Tories. A senior Conservative shows me their phone with a text from a week last Thursday [25th May] saying, 'We could go down to eight [seats]' So a week before polling it was clear it wasn't going well. They predict another election in six to twelve months.

08.30 The Liberal Democrats email with a response to their wipeout in Wales. 'This is a sad day for liberalism in Wales. Wales has lost a true liberal voice in Westminster, a voice fighting for a more open, tolerant country.'

08.45 As the rain holds off, Andrew RT Davies comes to me to give his reaction. 'It hasn't been a good night at the office for us,' he says, 'but we've got a bigger share of the overall vote – the biggest share in eighty years.' I ask him if he should resign. 'We all need to reflect on the result,' he says.

As for what went wrong: 'I would like to have seen a far more localised campaign here in Wales, a Welsh Conservative campaign because we know, if you look at the local government results in

May of this year when we had record-breaking results, when we run campaigns in Wales we succeed.'

So I ask him if Alun Cairns should consider his position. He only says, 'It's not for me to draw up the cabinet.'

10.00 I'm just about to try to grab some sleep when a Welsh Conservative source calls with a prepared statement. I scribble it down in pencil on several sheets of hotel notepaper and say, 'This is explosive.' 'Yes,' they reply. There were expletives but the gist was that Andrew should not take the blame. I tweet it as a thread with the warning: 'Stand by for some explosive words from a Welsh Conservatives source on the election campaign,' then turn my phone on silent.

This is what I scrawled onto the hotel notepaper:

There are serious questions to those responsible for devising the non-existent "Welsh election strategy." It's astonishing that we weren't given sight of the final manifesto before its publication. Andrew was proactively replaced on the Saturday night before the [BBC Wales] Ask the Leader debate. The Assembly group was effectively silenced, muted. We were told not to issue any lines on Labour or Plaid at the campaign. Contrast that forcibly with the successful 2015 campaign which was run with a Team Wales approach and the skill of Westminster and Assembly colleagues which resonated well with the voters.

I sleep for half an hour or so and turn my phone on.

Geraint won't comment on the explosive briefing, saying, 'It's not my style. It'll come out in the wash.' He says Alun hasn't heard anything yet about continuing as Secretary of State.

I text the Conservative MP I saw with his bags for life at the start of the campaign who says, 'Looks to me that anti-Tory voters in Wales took fright and voted Labour to stop us. Our poor organisation in key seats also cost us.' He adds that we 'wanted some certainty nationally and that we have definitely not got.'

A Labour AM tells me, 'It seems the Remain voters went for Labour, people liked Carwyn and they saw Jeremy wasn't a monster. Social media played its biggest role this time after several false starts. We didn't need to spend much on advertising on Facebook because people were doing it themselves.'

A Labour MP hints at problems to come in the parliamentary party. 'Jeremy is a very good campaigner but as a parliamentary leader he's a problem.' But, I reply, he's quite affable isn't he? 'He can be very passive aggressive.'

A senior Conservative tells me, 'There were some perverse results. We had no inkling that Labour could have taken Vale of Glamorgan or Aberconwy. Looking at Wrexham and Newport West, it's clear the ex-Labour UKIP voters have gone back to Labour.

'The manifesto was a big challenge. People found the manifesto a challenge. They were a bit pissed off.'

'The PM has done the right thing to stay on.'

Neil Hamilton tells my colleague James that, 'We knew there was going to be a massive squeeze of tactical voting and that seems to have happened to all the other parties as well.' James asks him if he'll be a candidate in the contest to replace Paul Nuttall. 'No.'

Owain interviews Leanne Wood in the incongruously calm setting of Aberaeron's harbour. She's gone there to highlight Plaid's surprise capture of Ceredigion and says, 'On what was a very difficult, polarising night, to win here in Ceredigion and to get the same number of MPs that Plaid Cymru has had on our best ever showing is not too bad a result for us at all.'

Meanwhile I've been travelling to London. In Westminster, Abingdon Green is packed with reporters, producers, camera operators in and out of tents or clambering up and down the big platforms of the BBC and Sky. Andrea and a team from the Cardiff newsroom are already there. So is Roger, who's being interviewed by every outlet. I grab the chance for a last chat about the election campaign and polling in a Facebook live.

On air at six o'clock, Andrea interviews Andrew RT Davies live down the line from his farm in the Vale of Glamorgan. He says the election was far from a disaster because, 'Our overall share of the vote has gone up considerably,' but acknowledges a 'disappointing night.' He tells Andrea that in the 'five weeks between positive local government results and the General Election, something dramatic happened that made sure Labour's vote went up dramatically and that allowed them to take seats away from us.'

Back in the studio, Jon interviews Carwyn Jones and asks him if he won the election or was it Jeremy Corbyn? 'A bit of both,' answers the First Minister then goes on to analyse three strands: 'Firstly, the strength of the Welsh Labour brand which many people on the doorstep picked up on and they liked the manifesto. Secondly Jeremy and his energy, the fact that he went around Britain, that he listened to people and he energised young people. And thirdly the disastrous campaign that the Tories ran. They ran a personality cult around Theresa May and we saw it come crashing down yesterday.'

On the votes of younger people, Carwyn Jones says, 'Young people decided they want their voices heard. That voice will not be silenced, it must lead to something tangible.'

Jon reminds the First Minister that seven weeks ago he'd said, 'Jeremy has to prove himself.'

'He's proved himself as a leader and a campaigner and someone who has broad appeal. All those tests have been satisfied.'

Back in Westminster I describe the election as one of those times when, like a Kaleidoscope or an Etch-A-Sketch, everything gets shaken up and starts again. This was supposed to be an election to end uncertainty but it's just created more.

Andrea asks me if I think there'll be another election in a few months. 'Oh I hope so,' I joke. 'But what do I know? I don't know anything.' With that, I throw my book in the air, alarming a German TV presenter further down our row of TV live positions. Andrea stifles a laugh, I look down at my shoes like a naughty schoolboy. Andrea's professionalism gets her through to the end of the programme. I look over at my now-battered red book lying on the grass of Abingdon Green. It seems an appropriate way to end.

AFTERWORD

It was early morning in Manchester. On the street someone was whistling loudly and tunefully 'Give me oil in my lamp keep me burning.' I couldn't see who. It was sunny and cold. With its red brick and sandstone buildings, some stained and dark, others steam-cleaned and bright, all of them jostling against shiny modern buildings, Manchester was going about its early business.

A man in a red beret was saying to an older man in a blue blazer with brass buttons, 'Excuse me, I must let off steam.' Then he shouted something indistinct. WASPI women protestors were setting up, some dressed as suffragists and trying out whistles and horns for later use.

The police were relaxed but there was certainly a large number of them. As well as the yellow-jacketed officers, there were armed police in black jackets and liaison officers in blue coats who were mingling with protestors and talking to them.

They were more noticeably active and willing to intervene than they seemed when the Conservative conference was held here two years ago. Then I was shouted at by angry protestors every time I went into the conference venue. Real anger: people leaning closely into my face and screaming 'Tory scum.' I tried to explain to one that I was a journalist but that only seemed to make them more angry.

This time around I was told that a number of Welsh Conservatives hadn't made the journey, put off by the abuse they received last time. There were certainly a lot of faces familiar to me who were missing this year and the conference hall was remarkably sparse remarkably often. I usually try to stand alongside a wall during conference speeches and anyway for the big names there are rarely any seats to be had. But when I walked into the hall ahead of a speech by Alun Cairns a steward came up to me, pointed to the seats arranged on the floor in front of the stage and said 'We're trying to fill up these seats before the raked seating so that it looks fuller, could you sit in one of these please?'

Conferences aren't the country and party memberships don't reflect the wider public. But both tell us a lot about wider trends and directions and reveal a great deal about the health and vitality or otherwise of a party. And in 2017, the UK conferences of the two main parties couldn't have had clearer messages for those of us who watch them.

Half-empty halls and half-demoralised members were the main characteristics of the Conservative conference in Manchester even before Theresa May's speech and nobody could have predicted that state of affairs at the beginning of the year or even at the beginning of the election. It was quite easy to forget sometimes that the party had won, or at least had come first, and was still in government.

The previous week in Brighton you could have been forgiven for thinking that the Labour party had won the election. The sense of euphoria was palpable. Business on the first day was delayed by over an hour because the queues to get into the Brighton Centre snaked all the way back along the sea front. On every street corner it seemed there were lines of people waiting to go into The World Tomorrow fringe events organised by Momentum. All day. Every day. There was seemingly constant selfie-taking. I even saw Ed Miliband being mobbed on a street corner by autograph hunters and people wanting selfies.

Every time I looked into the hall, it was full. My temporary desk in the conference venue was set up near an entrance to a balcony that I've never seen used. This year there was a steady stream of people looking for a sneaky way into the hall. After one of the big names spoke that stream became a flood. Every five minutes or so I'd hear coming from one of the TV monitors a speaker on the stage saying, 'My name is so and so; I'm a new member and this is my first time at conference,' followed by a huge cheer.

But if members seemed to be in control and celebrating, there was still dissent and disquiet. It was just muted. MPs were prevented from sitting in the seats on the conference hall and relegated to a balcony which prevented them from voting. There were still people who'd point out that Labour had just lost its third election in a row, but they did so privately. Some stayed away.

Last year's Welsh Night reception had been an awkward affair. Carwyn Jones and Jeremy Corbyn didn't seem to gel. Corbyn had just won a second leadership election and a large number of Welsh delegates had backed his opponent, the Pontypridd MP Owen

Smith. This year it looked like a bromance. With a broad smile, the First Minister said to laughter: 'Jeremy does have a very great weakness. He supports Arsenal.' Jones made fun too of Corbyn's reputation as a teetotal vegetarian, saying that when the two men met in the summer for lunch at Llanfairfechan he was nervous about what Corbyn would eat. 'I'm glad to say he had a plate of chips, so there are weaknesses in Jeremy's diet.' And this was from a man who just three months previously had warned that the same Jeremy had to prove himself.

Corbyn himself had mentioned the plate of chips when I'd interviewed him a few days earlier. I asked him if they'd discussed their differing views on post-Brexit single market membership during that lunch. He said, 'We did indeed. We shared chips and discussed Brexit. We looked at two pages on various websites. One of which said we were refusing to speak to each other, and the other one said we were in complete agreement. We decided we were in complete agreement.'

The unlikely bromance seems symbolic of a new dynamic. Welsh Labour leaders took the chance to build on internal rule changes and concerns about divisions and direction in the wider party to beef up autonomy in Wales. They won support from anti-Corbyn MPs who were glad of the chance to insulate the campaign in Wales from the party's unpopularity. Then when that started changing they were able to adapt the Welsh campaign to take advantage of the Corbyn surge.

Yet even at Welsh Night not everyone seemed signed up. One half of the large room felt like a rally: cheers, applause, selfies and singing (with a specific Welsh twist: Tonia Antoniazzi brought specially-made gin from her brother's wedding and led the crowd in a chorus of Oh Jeremy Cor-gin.) On the other side of the room conversations carried on regardless of the whoops and cheers around the platform. Labour's problems remain and will need to be resolved but from what I saw in Brighton it's a party that's renewed and reinvigorated, infused by the enthusiasm and energy of its new members and older hands who can't quite believe what's happening.

Since the election, politics hasn't really settled down. Theresa May's excruciatingly awkward speech seemed to encapsulate all her problems and those of her party. At the time of writing she appeared to have seen off an immediate threat to her leadership. A Conservative MP told me there was a determination amongst most in the party at Westminster to keep her in place for as long as possible because there was no agreement about an alternative. It won't stop some from agitating over the coming months or years.

As for the Welsh Conservatives there are again rumours about dissatisfaction towards Andrew RT Davies and making an effort to unseat him. The row over the TV debates and his attempt to bring UKIP defector Mark Reckless into the Tory group are the reasons which keep being raised for why he should go. Yet there seems little sense of momentum behind any challenger and he has his own grounds for resentment against other parts of the Tory leadership in Wales and in London. I don't get the sense that it's a happy party at either end of the M4.

Labour clearly is much happier than it was but it's not at all obvious what happens to it next. Polls suggest that it could win an election if one were held now, another reason keeping Theresa May in position. Welsh Labour's celebrating what now looks like the good sense of running a dual campaign but at the time looked like desperation followed by surprise. It is true however that Carwyn Jones has emerged strengthened from it which raises the question about when or whether he will step down as leader and First Minister. He'll have been in the job for ten years in 2019 and there are hints that he might be thinking about beginning a transition to a successor. And yet in many ways he's at his peak politically as First Minister and Welsh Labour leader and there's no sign of a challenger. Perhaps he'll see Brexit out and try to emulate Rhodri Morgan by leaving at a time of his choosing.

As I write elsewhere, Plaid Cymru is at or near a point of decision. Its constitution allows for a leadership election in 2018 but Leanne Wood may want to force one earlier than that date. Either way the party is thinking about the Assembly election in 2021 and has to decide if it continues with the direction she's set or tries another. Forcing Neil McEvoy to leave the group and ending its compact with Labour looks like a clearing of the decks for whatever happens next.

What all the parties have to face is difficulty and uncertainty. Budgets will continue to be tight forcing politicians and all levels to make unpalatable decisions. And the Brexit talks show no clear sign of what Britain will be like once we've left the EU. As well as the huge changes it'll create, the ripples are uncountable, including the effects it'll have on devolution which is in the process of changing anyway. The first Welsh taxes are now coming into being and will be followed by sharing control of income tax from 2018. The Assembly too will gain new powers including the ability to change its name to Welsh Parliament. I can't see that not happening. I'm certain too that sixteen- and seventeen-year-olds will be allowed to vote in Welsh elections fairly soon. The only certainty for the coming months and years is uncertainty. The only prediction is more change. It's a good job that I already have enough material to start a second volume. Everything has changed.

October 2017

ROCKING
THE BOAT
WELSH WOMEN WHO
CHAMPIONED EQUALITY
1840-1990
ANGELA V. JOHN

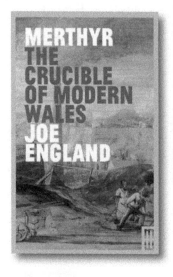

MERTHYR
THE
CRUCIBLE
OF MODERN
WALES
JOE
ENGLAND

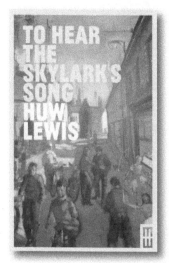

TO HEAR
THE
SKYLARK'S
SONG
HUW
LEWIS

A
Wilder
WALES

TRAVELLERS' TALES
1610-1831
DAVID
LLOYD
OWEN

PARTHIAN

www.parthianbooks.com

Lightning Source UK Ltd.
Milton Keynes UK
UKHW03f1531050418
320581UK00001B/47/P